COLLECTOR'S GUIDE TO

...BATTERIES NOT INCLUDED

IDENTIFICATION
& VALUES

DON HULTZMAN

COLLECTOR BOOKS
A Division of Schroeder Publishing Co., Inc.

The current values in this book should be used only as a guide. They are not intended to set prices, which vary from one section of the country to another. Auction prices as well as dealer prices vary greatly and are affected by condition as well as demand. Neither the Author nor the Publisher assumes responsibility for any losses that might be incurred as a result of consulting this guide.

Searching for a Publisher?

We are always looking for knowledgeable people considered to be experts within their fields. If you feel that there is a real need for a book on your collectible subject and have a large comprehensive collection, contact Collector Books.

Cover design: Beth Summers
Book design: Michelle Dowling

Printed in the U.S.A. by Image Graphics, Inc., Paducah, KY

Additional copies of this book may be ordered from:

COLLECTOR BOOKS
P.O. Box 3009
Paducah, Kentucky 42002–3009
or
Don Hultzman
5026 Sleepy Hollow Rd.
Medina, OH 44256

@ $19.95. Add $2.00 for postage and handling.

CONTENTS

DEDICATION

This book is dedicated to Barbara, Scott, Todd, Kurt, Kathryn, Sheri, Lauren, and Kyle.

ABOUT THE AUTHOR

Don Hultzman admits he has always been a casual collector of old toys, but didn't really get serious about the hobby until twenty or so years ago when he found that repairing broken toys was just as exciting as collecting them. Not only was he intrigued by these mechanical wonders, he also enjoyed the challenge of bringing a "dead" toy back to "life." These resurrections began with the classic tin wind-ups and later, the battery-operated toys. Currently, he is still an obsessive collector and repairer of mechanical toys, both battery-operated and wind-ups.

Born, raised, and educated in Cleveland, Ohio, he graduated from West Tech High School and then went on to Baldwin-Wallace College where he earned his bachelor of science degree. After a two-year stint in the Navy, he joined the Parma City School System as a science teacher. Later, he became a guidance counselor after earning his master's degree from Kent State University, Kent, Ohio.

Presently, he lives in Brunswick Hills, Ohio, a few miles south of Cleveland, and remains a staunch Indians fan.

Besides working, raising a family, and collecting and repairing toys, Don also did free-lance writing for the encyclopedia department of the World Publishing Company, as a science consultant. He also writes feature articles for toy publications as well as books on battery-operated toys. Many pieces from his extensive collection of pre-1960 tin wind-up toys were used in the 1983 MGM movie "A Christmas Story," and also the 1994 movie, "My Summer Story," also by MGM.

The author welcomes inquiries and can be reached at his home address:

5026 Sleepy Hollow Rd.
Medina, Ohio 44256

Please enclose an S.A.S.E. for a prompt response.

BATTERY TOY CLUB

For anyone interested in collecting battery toys, there is a non-profit organization devoted to advanced as well as beginning collectors of these toys.

Known as "Battery-Operated Toy Collectors of America" or "BOTCA" for short, this unique club is open to anyone, anywhere in the world, who would enjoy sharing and exchanging ideas, interests, and information, as well as keeping up on the latest in the battery toy world via a newsletter, Internet, fax, or just plain phone conversation. For more information, please contact:

Jack Smith
410 Linden
P.O. Box 676
Tolono, IL 61880

Please enclose an S.A.S.E. for a prompt response.

ACKNOWLEDGMENTS

Writing and publishing a book about those clever little automatons powered by batteries is a fascinating venture into the realm of fantasy and real life. Not only is this venture a pleasure, it is also a culmination of much work and research, compiling a vast amount of information; finalizing it; and reproducing it in book form for all to enjoy, learn about, and appreciate the world of battery-operated toys.

Toy collectors of all ages, from the Depression babies to the Baby Boomers, will find this book an informative and nostalgic trip back to those childhood memories when toys, all kinds of toys, represented the pleasant moments of growing up, along with those important and memorable occasions such as Christmas morning, birthdays, and other special holidays where toys brought out the smiles.

Looking back at those moments helps us go forward with a better idea of who we are and what is important to us, and the world of toys was a very important part of this concept — especially those battery operated toys!

To capture this nostalgia permanently, in print and photographs, involves a great deal of soliciting knowledge, compiling information, organizing facts, visual representations, and publication. To accomplish this end I would like to express my gratitude to the following folks who helped make this book possible:

To Richard O'Brien, who is perpetually up to his neck in his "Collecting" series of books on toys, cars and trucks, soldiers, trains, and great novels, but always manages to find time to be a constant source of advice and encouragement. Many, many thanks.

To my longtime friend, George Tissen, who first introduced me to the world of toys. I will always appreciate this and his bon mots.

To another longtime friend, Dale Jerkins, who jump-started me into the world of battery toys, I will always owe him a fresh supply of batteries.

To Dan Alexander, former publisher, for giving me the opportunity to "get my feet wet," in the book publishing world. I am deeply indebted.

To Jim Bunte, former editor of "Collecting Toys," for his encouragement and acceptance of my writings for his toy magazine, I will never forget.

To Ron Smith, old friend and "travel companion," I'm indebted for all I've learned about anything with "wheels" or "wings", and if he couldn't fill me in, then I depended on Rich and Faith Savage to continue the learning process as they have a wealth of knowledge to share anytime I needed it. To all, much appreciation.

To Ron Chojnacki, art teacher and "travel buddy," who did the brunt of the photographs in this book, I owe a bundle of thanks for a job well done.

To Boyd Stewart, old friend and transplanted Hoosier, goes a round of plaudits for many of the hard-to-find toys in this book. Thanks again for helping me share these finds with the rest of the world.

To Allan Milewski, D.D.S., goes the "Crowning Glory" award for keeping me in smiles, and dental tools to help keep those toys going, and going, and going.

To Rick Koch and John Lawson, who are my "Baby Boomerabilia" insiders, and have been very informative with the doings of the "plastic world," I give a hearty "Yaba Daba Doo," and thank you.

To Herb and Barb Smith of Smith House Toys, and Marty and Debbie Krim of the New England Auction Gallery, goes a lot of credit for helping me track down information on numerous toys through their excellent catalogs. Many, many thanks.

Many thanks and much appreciation go to the "deans" of all battery toy collectors, Arno and Anny Seeliger of Reading, Pa. You name it, and they either have it or will tell you all about it — in Pennsylvania Dutch, of course. Danke Schön, Arno and Anny.

My appreciation to Lisa Stroup, editor, Collector Books, Schroeder Publishing Co., and Billy Schroeder, publisher, for giving me the opportunity to get this book off the ground, after many setbacks.

To Jim Gelarden, set director for MGM Studios, and their use of my classic tin toys in the 1983 movie, "A Christmas Story" and the 1994 movie, "My Summer Story," goes a battery operated "Oscar."

To Ken Burkholder, Adam Zidek, John Scott, Tom Lastrapes, Al Schlesinger, Scott and Brynne Shaw, Dave Stanley, Jack Smith, Asa Sparks, and Jeff Bub, who provided me with a lot of useful information. Thanks, gang.

Last, but not least and, in case I've forgotten someone, thanks to all who fed me information from here, there, and everywhere that helped make this book a reality!

PHOTO CREDITS

Supplementing over 1,600 toy listings in this book are 300 plus photographs, from my collection and the private collections of many other battery toy enthusiasts.

It is with sincere appreciation and admiration I say a huge thank you for permitting me to share your pride and joy with the rest of the toy world.

Whether it be one photo or many photos, the following contributors have made this book a much improved and more comprehensive guide:

Jonathon Barrow
Paul Capito
Dave Conlin
Tom Duffy
Ira Eckstein
Bruce Hertzberg
Randy Ibey
Marty Krim
Victor Rodriguez
Perry Rotwein
Mike Sarisky
Tom Scalise
Arno Seeliger
Scott Shaw
Al Schlesinger
Herb Smith
Jack Smith
Ron Smith
Peter Yoss

INTRODUCTION

During the years preceding World War II, the Japanese toy industry was mainly concerned with making cheap, low cost imitations of American and European toys, mostly out of recycled tin cans and celluloid. These toys were simple, cheap, crude and not too desirable, resulting in a limited market for this type of export.

With the advent of WWII, Japan's involvement doomed all domestic manufacturing, including the toy industry, where all materials and manpower were now diverted to the war effort. The manufacture and export of these sleazy toys were now temporarily terminated.

Following WWII and Japan's defeat, Japanese technology was drastically curtailed and restricted by the terms of the peace treaty, one of which strictly prohibited the manufacture of anything related to war or the military.

This left Japan with a large surplus of brain power that that had been occupied by its futile war effort.

In order to overcome the economic devastation of WWII and survive, Japanese engineers, scientists, and manufacturers had to focus on a new and untapped market for unique, different, and high quality products. With these prime objectives, and diversity in mind, the Japanese succeeded in many areas, such as automotives, optical, electronics, and toys.

During this period immediately after the war and through the 1960s, the Japanese came into their own with a new and different dimension in the world of toys — the concept of the battery-operated toy.

EARLY BATTERY TOYS

Previously, early U.S. and European toy makers used batteries in their toys to add realism to their boats, cars, trains, and airplanes by adding flashlight bulbs where headlights, spotlights, tail-lights and navigation lights were required. Later, batteries were used to power horns, buzzers, and electromagnets as well as light bulbs, but these early mechanical toys still depended on a spring or small flywheel to function as a mechanical toy should. There was just so much these early toys could do until the Japanese toy revolution opened up a whole new area with its clever automatons.

LATER BATTERY TOYS

Starting in the late 40s, Japanese toy makers began to replace the wind-up clockwork mechanisms and friction-drive mechanical toys with miniature electric motors powered by one or more batteries. These small electric motors could run much longer than the spring powered or friction-drive mechanisms and, with this advantage, the Japanese toy makers designed and manufactured the most ingenious and complicated toys imaginable. They were able to simulate just about every conceivable type of human-animal motion and behavioral action. This ingenuity carried over into a multitude of different types of novelty toys. Just how many different types of automata and vehicles were manufactured is unknown, but a conservative estimate would be around the 2,000 mark. Multiply this figure by the thousands and it was no wonder that Japan held the title of the leading toy maker and exporter for the next 20 years. About 95% of the battery-operated toys came from Japan during this period while the U.S. and other countries manufactured the remaining 5% of these toys.

HOW THEY GOT HERE

Since most of the Japanese production was destined for the U.S. and European markets, international distributorships were organized for the marketing of these thousands of toys. Cragstan, Linemar, Rosko and Illfelder were some of the largest international distributors, but a few American toy makers hopped on the band wagon, marketing these toys under their brand names, such as Marx, Ideal, Hubley and Daisy (the BB gun people). Therefore, many of the trademarks stamped on Japanese battery-

operated toys are not necessarily those of the original manufacturer, but of the distributor or marketer. Many Japanese cottage industry toy shops and factories manufactured, assembled and sold their products through a central factory which in turn was under contract to an international marketer. As a result, it is very difficult to pinpoint a specific designer or manufacturer of any battery-operated toy.

All the toys listed in this guide are of Japanese origin, unless otherwise noted.

WHO MADE THEM

Some of the early Japanese toy makers, such as the Masutoku Toy Factory (later Masudaya Toy Co.), founded in 1924 (used the M-T or Modern Toy trademark) and Nomura Toys, Ltd., founded in 1923 (used the T-N trademark), are probably two of the original designers and manufacturers of many of the hundreds of different automatons exported from Japan. Alps Shoji, Ltd., (Alps Toy Midzuno Co., trademark Alps), founded in 1948 and Marusan Co., (trademark SAN), founded in 1946, can also be documented as creators of many original battery toys. In fact, Marusan Co. and Bandai, founded in 1950, as well as the Taijo Kogyo Co., founded in 1959, can be credited with some of the most spectacular scale model, battery-operated cars ever made in that category. Ashai Toy Co., founded in 1950 (trademark ATC), Toplay Ltd., founded in 1956 (trademark T.P.S.), and the Mansei Toy Co., founded in 1951 (trademark Haji), have their trademarks on many more toys. The alphabet soup continues with many other toy companies using only a single letter or letters like "K", "S", "J", "KO", "Y", and "S&E", etc. A good example is the Yonezawa Co., which uses the "YONE" trademark as well as the single letter "Y" on a lot of its toys. Why only letters is a mystery, unless they represent many subsidiaries of the parent company. Besides being clever, the Japanese have left toy collectors very confused, but this is a small disadvantage compared to the fun of collecting battery-operated toys.

THE GOLDEN AGE

It is generally agreed upon by battery-operated toy collectors that the period of the 1940s – 60s should be considered the "Golden Age of Battery-Operated Toys". During this 20-year period, most of the quality toy companies were founded, and the most desirable and beautiful toys were produced. They were high in quality, complex, and fascinating in their detail and lithography. These toys are the ones most sought after and in demand today. Prices of these toys are generally increasing as they become more scarce, and more and more toy collectors are beginning to focus on their desirability and are willing to pay as much for them as they have for many of the early classic tin wind-ups. Top prices go for the most complex toys, comic characters, space, robots, scale-model cars, Blacks, and the older and earlier figurals. The "Ball Playing Bear" is a good example of one of the first batt-op toys of the late 40s. As in most early toys, it uses one D-cell, is made of tin and celluloid, has six actions going on, and is very difficult to find complete with all its accessories.

MORTALITY RATE

Although tens of thousands of battery-operated toys were in circulation during this period, it is a rarity and a thrill to find one in mint condition, with original box, as the mortality rate of these toys was extremely high. Corrosion from leaking batteries left in them by absent-minded owners took a high toll as well as deterioration of rubber parts due to age. (Rubber hoses of the water-drinkers and the rubber bellows of the bubble blowers were classic victims of aging and hardening of the rubber.) Rust was inevitable with the wet-toys that depended on water or bubble solutions to perform. Lubricants dried out or stiffened, rendering the toy inoperable, wires frequently worked loose or broke, and electrical contacts corroded. Accidents, abuse, tampering, and interfering with the toy while it was going through its cycle added enormously to the mortality rate. Reversing battery polarity, by not following instructions, burned out and ruined many a fine toy. Like a precision watch, the more complex the toy, the more delicate the mechanism and the more susceptible it becomes to damage due to negligence and abuse. Physically interfering with the actions of the toy, and stopping it before it completes its cycle will damage the many levers and gears inside the toy, making it useless. Many toys require accessory parts to perform correctly, such as bowls for the bubble-blowers, trays, balls, umbrellas, discs, flags, clothes, etc., and these were often lost. Top prices usually go for complete toys with no parts missing.

THE ORIGINAL BOX

The original box for battery-operated toys is extremely important, probably more so than other mechanical toys, because the instructions were often printed on the box lid. Also a picture or illustration of the toy showing any accessory parts the toy might need, as well as the correct battery insertion, was noted if not printed on the toy's battery compartment. Finally, the name of the toy, if not lithographed on the toy itself, was printed on the box and very often this printed name was nothing near the name appearing on the toy. Many times the name of the toy was given for its function rather than what it was supposed to be, and since many toys did not have their identity stamped on them, the box lid was the only means of identifying the toy. The toy listings that follow are names of toys actually identified from their original boxes or from the toy itself. Therefore, the original box usually adds significantly to the value of the toy.

The original boxes had a higher mortality rate than the toys, especially on Christmas morning as the Baby Boomers tore into their presents and the toys took priority over the boxes the toys came in. Ultimately the boxes wound up in the trash can. Very few kids or parents at the time had the slightest concept of the value of the box and why it should be kept. They could care less about saving them and, besides, they took up a lot of room — so out they went.

A small percentage of the original boxes and toys did survive and are today's collectibles. Presently, most of the toys and boxes on the market come from warehouse finds, attics, defunct variety stores, and obsessive collectors who hoarded and saved everything.

VALUE OF THE BOX

Establishing the value of the original box depends on many variables such as:
1. The value of the toy minus its box.
2. Condition of the box.
3. Graphics on the box lid.
4. Type of information on box lid.
5. Rarity of the toy and/or box.
6. Importance of box to toy owner.

Also the box should be complete with a lid (top) and a bottom, or it may consist of a single piece with flaps. The lid usually contains the graphics and information and is the most important part. The box bottom is usually plain cardboard and, by itself, adds no value to the toy, other than as a container for the toy. The original inserts may add some value to the box.

The original box could add as little as 10% to the value of the toy or as much as 100%, doubling the value of a very rare toy.

CALCULATING THE VALUE OF A BOX

To get an approximate idea of the value of the complete box, it is suggested that the Rarity number be multiplied by 10%. This percentage times the value of the toy will give an approximation of the value of the toy and its original box. This value will never be absolute because as the law of supply and demand changes, so will the rarity and value of any toy. The bottom line is that the value of any toy and/or box will be the final negotiated price between buyer and seller.

NOTE:
THE VALUES OF THE BATTERY TOYS LISTED IN THIS GUIDE ARE FOR THE TOYS ONLY, WITHOUT THE ORIGINAL BOXES, SINCE MOST TOYS EXIST THIS WAY.

PRODUCTION DECLINES

After peaking in the late 60s, the Japanese tin toy production began to decline due to increased labor costs, increased safety restrictions, inflation, and competition from the cheaper die-cast and plastic toy makers. Many of the original toy companies either folded or diversified into the electronic field, using the IC-microchip the same way they used the mini-electric motor to develop new electronic products. It seems that currently Japan has relinquished its toy monopoly to China, Hong Kong, Korea, and Taiwan in favor of its automotive and electronic industry. The battery-operated toys now coming from these countries consist mostly of plastic, are high priced, lack quality, and are presently not very collectible. There is no comparison to the beauty of these toys with those from Japan. Tin and plastic have never been compatible in a quality toy and this combination tends to turn off most serious toy collectors.

MAJOR AND MINOR ACTIONS

The value of a battery-operated toy depends not only on its scarcity, desirability, and condition, but also on the number of actions taking place during its performance cycle. These toys are classified as major or minor action toys. Major action toys will have three or more actions taking place while performing and will command top price, while minor action toys have only one or two actions and will have a correspondingly lower price. The actions of a major or minor toy include all the individual movements taking place during one cycle and include any lights, sounds, or smoke effects. Also the major battery toys must have all actions functioning and occurring in proper sequence. There should be no missing parts and the toy itself should be constructed mostly of tin, about 85-90%, with the rest plastic or vinyl, such as heads, limbs, accessories, etc. Usually the more plastic, the lower the value of the toy, regardless of condition.

This book's listing of battery-operated toys is, for the most part, major action toys, and include, if known, the manufacturer or distributor derived from the box or lithographed on the toy itself. A "?" indicates that the name of this toy has not been verified by the author. Also production year, if known, will follow, along with the most obvious or helpful dimensions and any special notes. The prices are the average market prices based on supply and demand, and not on auction or "will pay anything for this toy" price. Geographic area is another factor used in pricing and prices given here were based on the going prices in the midwestern states.

RARITY SCALE

The rarity scale is an indicator of the general availability of battery-operated toys. Since only a limited number of battery toys survived the "Golden Age," it stands to reason that as more and more new battery toy collectors enter the hobby, the general availability of these toys becomes drastically decreased. As the law of supply and demand takes over, the prices of the rarer toys will go nowhere but up — if they can be found at all, on the open market.

The rarity scale is based on a continuum of 1 to 10. A toy with a rarity of 1 is extremely common and easy to find. As the rarity number increases, the toys get more difficult to find and, as the rarity number approaches a 10, the toy is so scarce that it seems to be non-existent. **The rarity number appears at the right of the value range.**

Since the rarity scale is an indicator of scarcity and desirability, it follows that as the number increases, so will the price of a certain rare toy.

A rare toy is one that is difficult to find on the open market because: 1. It had a limited production; 2. It is of such a fragile nature that it is difficult to find complete or in operating condition; or 3. It is so popular and highly collectible that it appears only in private collections.

GUIDELINES FOR THE CARE AND REPAIR OF YOUR BATTERY-OPERATED TOY

Your prized battery toy needs a lot of "T.L.C." and when it stops working, you have a frustrating disaster on your hands. To avoid this, the following suggestions should help:

Battery toys, like other mechanical toys, should be operated periodically to keep them loosened up. A lightweight spray lubricant used now and then will help considerably if the mechanism is accessible. Do not over-lubricate because the excess may stain any cloth or fur covering on some battery toys.

A good quality car wax or polish will keep the lithographed and bare metal parts looking like new — especially on the wet toys. Always test an obscure lithographed area to make sure the polish doesn't soften or dissolve the paint. Care should be exercised when polishing metal parts adjoining any cloth or plush covering since the substance may stain the coverings. Light surface rust usually disappears with a careful polishing. Nothing can be done for deep rust or corrosion without ruining the value of the toy. Repainting will only further reduce the value and is not recommended.

Should your battery toy fail to operate, the following steps might be helpful:

1. Make sure it is not gunked-up and that no moving parts are binding.

2. Make sure the battery contacts are not dirty or corroded — if so then clean them with crocus cloth. Always used fresh batteries!

3. Lightly tap the toy with your finger or gently nudge one of the moving parts while the switch is on.

If none of the above steps works, your toy needs major surgery. This means the toy must be completely disassembled, repaired, and reassembled. Most battery toys are repairable as long as they have not been destructively tampered with and no parts are missing or corroded beyond repair. This job is best left to an expert in toy repair and should never be attempted by one who doesn't know what he is doing. Expert repairs will not affect the value of a battery toy as long as the repair is undetectable and the toy looks and functions exactly as it did before the repair. Such repairs are acceptable in toy collecting circles. Expert repairs are also expensive but well worth the investment if it means the difference between a prized toy and one that no longer functions since an inoperable toy is practically worthless, (regardless of condition) because it is no longer a toy, only an expensive display piece.

Finally, keep in mind that these toys were not designed to be repaired, and one simple mishap could easily ruin a favorite toy. Take good care of your toys and they will give you many more years of pleasure.

TROUBLE SHOOTING GUIDE
Common Problems of Battery-Operated Toys

Problem	Causes
1. Light Works — No Action	1. Wire detached from motor. Burned-out motor.
2. Motor Works — No Action	2. Plastic pinion cracked and slipping on motor shaft. Also defective drive gears.
3. Smoking toy won't smoke	3. Dry or burned-out smoke generator. Weak batteries. Loose wires.
4. No air coming out of bubble or balloon-blowing toys	4. Holes or cracks in rubber or paper bellows. Also holes or cracks in rubber hoses.
5. Motor makes screeching noise	5. Dry motor bearings. Needs oil.
6. Some actions not working	6. Defective cams, gears or rods. Shaft slippage.
7. Intermittent actions	7. Loose, but not detached, wire connections. Cold solder connections. Needs resoldering.
8. Toy is turned on, runs, and suddenly stops	8. Gears jammed, batteries inserted incorrectly.
9. Dead toy — no action	9. Dirty contacts, corroded battery terminals. Loose wires, weak or incorrectly inserted batteries, jammed gears. Motor burned out.

NOTE: In all cases make sure batteries are fresh and inserted properly before declaring a battery toy a DISASTER!

TOY CONDITION AND VALUE

The value of a battery-operated toy depends not only on its desirability, rarity, and complexity, but very much on its condition. Since there are so many variables and interpretations regarding the condition of a toy, this guide will address itself to the conditions most important to dealers and collectors — very good and excellent. **The first value applies to a toy in very good condition which is generally worth about half as much as a toy in excellent condition. The second value then applies to a toy in excellent condition.**

The key to determining the value and condition of any toy is to use common sense and avoid wishful thinking. Since pricing and determining the condition of a toy may be difficult at times, consulting an experienced collector or dealer, if possible, could clear up any lingering doubts or confusion. The following explanations of very good and excellent may be helpful:

VERY GOOD

Very good indicates the condition of a battery toy that has seen some use and is starting to show its age. It will still be in perfect working order and have all its accessory parts where applicable. It will have some age-soiling, but will have no rust or corrosion. Overall, it will have an appearance of freshness and still be highly desirable to the fussy collector.

EXCELLENT

Excellent, like new or mint means just that — the condition in which the toy was originally issued — perfect — regardless of age. It will also be complete with all accessory parts when applicable, and will look brand new. The cloth or fur (plush) covering on some battery toys may reveal some discoloration (yellowing) due to age, but this should not affect its value as a mint toy as long as it is clean. All toys in this category must be in perfect working condition. The original box, in mint condition, will significantly enhance the value of any mint toy.

Any battery toy below the condition of very good will reflect a drastic reduction in value. Toys in good shape but missing accessory parts will not lose as much value as those that are severely rusted, corroded, painted over, have parts broken, and are totally inoperable. These poor toys are usually collected for their scrap value by the toy repairer and seldom are they worth more than a few dollars.

Note: Occasionally a toy will show evidence **of factory touch-up paint, especially around the tabs, edges, or corners of the toy. This is acceptable and will have no effect on the value.**

WORDS OF WISDOM

Please keep in mind that this guide is just that — a guide. Book values are not firm, but relative to many, many variables and can fluctuate at any time, any place, and any given moment.

To avoid disappointments in collecting battery-operated toys, you should

1. Collect only what you like since you'll have to live with your decision and purchase.

2. Collect and purchase only the best that you can afford and try to avoid the temptation of bargains.

3. Buy toys only because you like them. Buying toys for investment is not advisable and, like the stock market, is very risky.

A-B-C Fairy Train, 1950s, M-T Co., 14½" long, one piece, four actions

$80.00	$160.00	2

A-B-C Toyland Express, 1950s, M-T Co., 14½" long, four actions

$80.00	$160.00	3

Accordion Bear, 1950s, Y Co., 10½" tall, six actions

$220.00	$440.00	5

Accordion Bear, 1950s, Alps Co., 11" tall, five actions with remote microphone

$400.00	$800.00	9

Accordion Bear, 1950s, MST Co. (Flare Toy), 9¼" high, five actions

$140.00	$280.00	2

Accordion Playing Hobo with Musical Chimp, 1950s, Alps Co., 10" high, six actions

$250.00	$500.00	6

Accordion Playing Bunny with Baby Bunny Playing Cymbals, 1950s, Alps Co., 12" high, 9" long, six actions

$200.00	$400.00	6

Acro Chimp Porter, 1960s, Y-M Co., 8½" tall, minor toy

$50.00	$100.00	1

Acrobat Clown, 1960s, 9" tall, Y-M Co., minor toy

$60.00	$120.00	2

Acrobat Cycle, 1970s, Sunny Brand (Taiwan), 9" long, four actions, mostly plastic

$40.00	$80.00	3

Acrobat Robot, 1970s, S-H Co., 4½" tall, three actions

$50.00	$100.00	2

Adorable Daksy – The Obedient Dachshund, 1960s, Alps Co., 9" long, five actions, a.k.a. 'dorable Daksy

$30.00	$60.00	3

Aerial Ropeway, 1950s, T-N Co., 5" long, tin, cable-car, minor toy, includes a suspension rope and cardboard figures

$60.00 $120.00   3

Air Cargo Prop-Jet Airplane — Seaboard World Airlines, 1960s, Marx Co., 12" long, 14½" wingspan, five actions

$200.00 $400.00   6

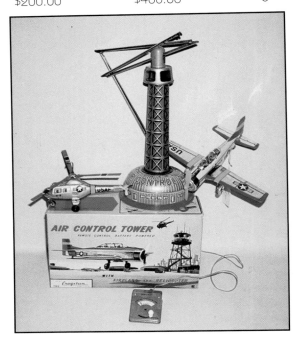

Air Control Tower, 1960s, Bandai Co., 11" high, 37" span (extended), four actions, includes detachable airplane and helicopter

$200.00 $400.00   4

Air Defense Truck with Lighted Pom-Pom Guns, 1950s, Line-mar Co., 14" long, five actions

$150.00 $300.00   5

Air Fighter With Bombing Action, 1960s, Bandai Co.,10" long, 8" wingspan, four actions, includes bombs and tank target

$130.00 $260.00   8

Air Fighting Pilot, 1950s, Bandai Co., 17" long, assembled, three actions

$120.00 $240.00   4

Air Force Rescue Battalion, (helicopter), 1950s, Marx Co., (Japan), 17" long, six actions, includes two tin rotors

$90.00 $180.00   7

Air Mail Helicopter, 1960s, K-O Co., 10" long, seven actions, includes detachable plastic rotor

$100.00 $200.00   4

Air Port Service Bus (VW Alitalia), 1950s, TT Co., 9½" long, minor toy

$90.00 $180.00   6

Air Taxi Helicopter, 1960s, Haji Co., three actions

$50.00 $100.00   3

Aircraft Carrier multi-action, 1950s, Marx Co., 20" long, six actions

$300.00 $600.00   7

Aircraft Carrier — Forrestal, 1950s, Linemar, 13¾" long, three actions, includes detachable plastic airplane

$200.00 $400.00   6

Airport Saucer, 1960s, M-T Co., 8" diameter, four actions

$90.00 $180.00   3

Airport Saucer, 1960s, S-T Co., four actions, 9" diameter

$100.00 $200.00   3

All Star Mr. Baseball Jr., see Mr. Baseball, Jr.

Alley — The Exciting New Roaring Stalking Alligator, 1960s, Marx Co., 17½" long, five actions

| $150.00 | $300.00 | 7 |

American Airlines – 4 Prop Airliner, 1960s, Waco Co., 12" long, 16½" wingspan, four actions

| $120.00 | $240.00 | 3 |

American Airlines DC-7 with sequential spinning propellers, c.1950s, Linemar, seven actions, 19" wingspan

| $200.00 | $400.00 | 4 |

American Airlines Airliner DC-7, multi-action, 1960s, Yonezawa Co., 21" long, 23½" wingspan, seven actions

| $190.00 | $380.00 | 4 |

American Airlines Airliner DC-7, 1960s, Linemar Co., 17½" long, 19" wingspan, seven actions

| $200.00 | $400.00 | 5 |

American Airlines Electra, 1950s, Linemar Co., 18" long, 19½" wingspan, four actions

| $200.00 | $400.00 | 5 |

American Airlines Flagship Caroline, 1950s, Linemar Co., 18" long, 19½" wingspan, three actions

| $190.00 | $380.00 | 4 |

American Circus Television Truck, 1950s, Exelo Co., 9¼" long, six actions, includes detachable metal antenna

| $600.00 | $1,200.00+ | 9 |

Amphibian Navy Patrol Plane with Flashing Lights, 1950s, Alps Co., 13" long, 15" wingspan, five actions

| $900.00 | $1,800.00 | 9 |

Amtrak Locomotive, 1960s, S-T Co., 16" long, minor toy

| $60.00 | $120.00 | 2 |

Andy Gard – Brink's Armored Car-Bank, 1950s, General Molds & Plastics Corp., 6¾" long, minor toy

| $40.00 | $80.00 | 2 |

Andy Gard Combat Knights No. 143, 1950s, General Molds & Plastics Corp., 10¼" high, three actions, includes lance, stanchion, three plastic rings, and helmet plume

| $80.00 | $160.00 | 6 |

Andy Gard Jaguar Sports Car, 1950s, General Molds & Plastics Corp., 9½" long, four actions, mostly plastic

| $70.00 | $140.00 | 3 |

Andy Gard – Telephone Truck, 1950s, General Molds & Plastics Corp., 6¾" tall, minor toy

| $50.00 | $100.00 | 4 |

Animated Santa Claus, 1950s, HTC Co., 10" tall, five actions, long chimney version

| $110.00 | $220.00 | 8 |

Animated Santa on Rotating Globe, 1950s, HTC Co., 15" high, five actions

| $400.00 | $800.00 | 5 |

Animated Squirrel, 1950s, S&E Co., 8½" tall, eight actions

| $100.00 | $200.00 | 3 |

Annie Tugboat, 1950s, Y Co., 12½" long, four actions
        $90.00 $180.00   **5**

Answer Game Machine, Robot, 1960s, Ichida Co., 14½" tall, educational toy, eight actions
        $300.00 $600.00   6

Anti-Aircraft Jeep, 1950s, K Co., 9½" long, five actions
        $100.00 $200.00   3

Anti-Aircraft Jeep, 1950s, T-N Co., 11" long, six actions, includes detachable tin radar antenna
        $150.00 $300.00   5

Anti-Aircraft Tank Firing Cannons M-75, 1950s, K Co., 9" long, five actions
        $50.00 $100.00   2

Anti-Aircraft Unit No. 1, 1950s, Linemar Co., 12½" long, three electrical actions and three manual actions
        $150.00 $300.00   4

Antique Fire Car, 1950s, T-N Co., 10" long, six actions
        $150.00 $300.00   4

Antique Gooney Car, 1960s, Alps Co., 9" long, four actions
        $70.00   **$140.00**   **2**

Apollo II-American Eagle Lunar Module, 1960s, DSK Co., 10" high, seven actions, includes detachable plastic antenna
        $200.00 $400.00   3

Apollo 11 Space Rocket, 1960s, T-N Co., 14" long, five actions
        $80.00   **$160.00**   **5**

Apollo Lunar Module, 1970s, DSK Co., 6" high, four actions, mostly plastic
        $170.00 $340.00   3

Apollo Saturn Two-Stage Moon Rocket, 1960s, T-N Co., 24" long, five actions
        $110.00 $220.00   5

Apollo Spacecraft, 1960s, Alps Co., 9" long, four actions, includes detachable plastic antenna
        $150.00 $300.00   5

Apollo Spacecraft, 1960s, M-T Co., 10" long, four actions, includes detachable astronaut
        $150.00 $300.00   5

Apollo Space Ship USA-NASA, 1960s, M-T Co., 9" long, four actions
        $70.00 $140.00   3

Apollo Super Space Capsule, 1960s, S-H Co., 9" high, five actions
        $100.00 $200.00   4

Apollo-X Moon Challenger, rocket, 1960s, T-N Co., 16" long, six actions
        $120.00 $240.00   5

Apollo Z Moon Traveler, 1960s, Alps Co., 9" long, 12" extended, five actions, includes detachable plastic antenna
$160.00 $320.00   5

Area Radiation Testor, space vehicle, 1950s, unmarked and distributed by Sears, 20" long, six actions
$400.00 $800.00   10

Armored Attack Set, 1960s, Marx Co., jeep, 6¼" long, plus 15-2" plastic figures, three actions
$200.00 $400.00   7

Army Radio Jeep – J1490, 1950s, Linemar Co., 7¼" long, four actions
$100.00 $200.00   4

Army Helicopter – Huey by Bell, 1960s, T-N Co., 10½" long, six actions
$90.00 $180.00   3

Army Train Set, 1950s, Haji Co., 15½" long, assembled, four piece train and six sections of track, minor toy
$100.00 $200.00   7

Arthur A-Go-Go-Drummer, 1960s, Alps Co., 10" high, six actions, includes detachable cymbals and lighted drum
$200.00 $400.00   5

Astro Captain, 1960s, Daiya Co., 6½" tall, three actions
$300.00 $600.00   5

Astro Dog, 1960s, Y Co., 11" high, two cycles, five actions, looks like Snoopy
$100.00 $200.00   3

Astro Dog, 1960s, Y-M Co., 11" tall, three actions
$90.00 $180.00   2

Astro Racer With Multi-Action, 1960s, Daiya Co., 12" long, four actions
$150.00 $300.00   5

Astrobase, motorized, Ideal Toy Co., 1960s, 21" high, 11" wide, six actions, includes rocket firing scout car and two plastic rockets
$180.00 $360.00   4

Astronaut – with space gun, 1960s, Daiya Co., 14" tall, five actions
$500.00 $1,000.00+   8

Astronaut, with walkie-talkie, 1960s, T-N Co., 13" tall, five actions, a.k.a. Blue or Red Rosko
$500.00 $1,000.00   3

Atom Motorcycle, see Expert Motor Cyclist

Atom Rocket-7, vehicle with fins, 1960s, M-T Co., 9½" long, four actions
$120.00 $240.00   5

Atom Rocket-15, Interplanetary Spaceship, 1960s, Y Co., 13½" long, four actions, includes detachable plastic antenna
$110.00 $220.00   6

Atomic Armored Train Set, 1950s, Bandai Co., 21½" long, assembled, minor toy, includes locomotive, three cars, 10 pieces of track and tin station

$150.00	**$300.00**	**7**

Atomic Boat, 1950s, Famous Co., minor toy, 15" long,

$150.00	$300.00	7

Atomic Fighter, robot, 1950s, S-H Co., 11" tall, five actions

$100.00	$200.00	5

Atomic Fire Car With Atomic Extinguisher, T-N Co., 1950s, 9½" long, four actions

$120.00	**$240.00**	**8**

Atomic Ray Gun, 1950s, M-T Co., 18" long, three actions

$90.00	$180.00	6

Atomic Reactor with Battery, 1950s, Linemar Co., 9" high, 12" long, three actions, includes plastic funnel and wrench

$110.00	$220.00	6

Atomic Rocket X-1800, 1960s, M-T Co., 9" long, three actions

$150.00	$300.00	4

Atomic Submarine, 1950s, Marx Co. (Japan), 13½" long, three actions, includes six plastic rockets

$100.00	$200.00	7

Attacking Martian Robot, 1950s, S-H Co., 11½" tall, seven actions, two cycles

$120.00	$240.00	3

Automatic Take-off and Landing Jet, 1950s, T-N Co., 11" long, 10" wingspan, TWA 707, five actions

$150.00	$300.00	6

Auto-Top Ferrari Convertible, 1960s, Bandai Co., 11" long, three actions

$450.00	$900.00	7

Auto Transport, 1950s, Linemar Co., 15" long, three actions, includes four tin cars

$150.00	$300.00	8

Automatic Space Viewer, picture gun & theater, 1950s, Stephens Co., 8" long, minor toy, with seven films in two boxes

$90.00	$180.00	7

Automatic Toll Gate, 1955, Sears, 16"x17" base, six actions, includes 8" tin Valiant car

$150.00	$300.00	4

Automated Santa, c.1960s, Santa Creations Co., 10" tall, three actions

$100.00	$200.00	6

B-52 Electronic Ball Turret Gun, 1950s, Remco Co., 25" long, six actions, mostly plastic

$100.00	$200.00	7

B-58 Hustler Jet, 1950s, Marx Co., 21" long, 12" wingspan, four actions

$450.00	$900.00+	7

Baby and Carriage with Pony Tail Girl, 1950s, S&E Co., 8½" long, 7" tall, four actions

$100.00	$200.00	5

Baby Bertha – The Watering Elephant, 1960s, Mego Corp., 10" high assembled, three actions, includes detachable tin flag

$100.00	$200.00	5

Baby Carriage, 1950s, T-N Co., 10" long, minor toy, includes plastic baby bottle to activate switch

$60.00	$120.00	4

Baby First Step – The Walking and Skating Doll, 1964, Mattel Co., 18" tall, minor toy, includes roller skates

$30.00	$60.00	6

Ball Blowing Clown, 1950s, T-N Co., 11" tall, three actions, with celluloid ball

$180.00	$360.00	4

Ball Playing Bear, 1940s, no marking, 10½" tall, six actions, includes five celluloid balls and one umbrella

$450.00	**$900.00**	**8**

Ball Playing Dog, 1950s, Linemar Co., 9" high, three actions

$120.00	$240.00	5

Balloon Blowing Monkey, 1950s, Alps Co., 11½" tall, six actions, with balloon

$120.00	$240.00	4

Balloon Poodle, 1960s, Y Co., 11" tall, two cycles, four actions

$60.00	$120.00	2

Balloon Vendor, 1960s, Y Co., 12" tall, four actions, includes four plastic balloons and tin tray

$130.00	$260.00	4

Baragon, 1960s, Bullmark Co., 10" tall, three actions

$290.00	$580.00	6

Barber Bear, 1950s, T-N Co., Linemar, 9½" tall, five actions

$300.00	**$600.00**	**4**

Barking Boxer Dog, 1950s, Marx, 7" long, minor toy

$50.00	$100.00	2

Barking Dog, 1950s, STS Co., 7" long, 7" high, four actions, two cycles

$50.00	$100.00	2

Barking Spaniel Dog, 1950s, Marx, 7" long, minor toy

$50.00	$100.00	2

Barking Shepherd Dog, 1950s, Marx, 7" long, three actions

$50.00	$100.00	4

Barney Bear – The Drummer Boy, 1950s, Alps Co., 11" tall, five actions, resembles Steiff bear

$130.00	$260.00	4

Barnyard Rooster, 1950s, Marx, 10" high, five actions

$100.00	$200.00	4

Bartender, 1960s, T-N Co., 11½" tall, six actions

$40.00	**$80.00**	**1**

Baseball Pitching Game, 1960s, Marx Co., 12½" long, minor toy

$100.00	$200.00	7

Batman, 1960s, T-N Co., 11½" tall, three actions

$500.00	$1,000.00+	10

Batmobile, 1960s, ASC Co., 9" long, remote control, three actions

$300.00	$600.00	5

Batmobile, 1972, National Periodical Publications, ASC Co., 12" long, three actions

$180.00	$360.00	2

Batmobile, 1970s, Taiwan, 10" long, three actions
$70.00 $140.00   2

Batmobile with Fire Lighted Engine, 1970s, ASC Co., 11" long, three actions
$300.00 $600.00   8

Battery Locomotive, 1950s, T-N Co., minor toy, 14" long, with tender
$50.00 $100.00   7

Battery Locomotive No. 123, 1950s, T-N Co., 10" long, three actions
$30.00 $60.00   1

Battery Operated Jet Plane, Pan American DC-7, 1950s, Linemar Co., 19¼" long, 18" wingspan, four actions, with sequential lighted engines
$170.00 $340.00   6

Battle Helicopter – U.S. Army N-41312, 1960s, Alps Co., 12" long, four actions, includes two detachable plastic rotors
$80.00 $160.00   6

Bear Chef (Cuty Cook), 1960s, Y Co., 9½" tall, five actions, includes chef hat and tin litho egg
$150.00 $300.00   6

Bear Target Game, 1950s, M-T Co., 8¾" high, 4" x 5" base, includes gun, rubber tipped darts, detachable drum, four actions
$200.00 $400.00   6

Bear – The Cashier, 1950s, M-T Co., 7½" high, five actions
$190.00 $380.00   6

Bear the Magician, 1950s, MTS Co., 12½" tall, nine actions
$1,000.00 $2,000.00+   9

Bear The Shoemaker, 1950s, T-N Co., 8½" high, three actions
$140.00 $280.00   5

Bear Typist, 1950s, T-N Co., 7½" high, seven actions
$400.00 $800.00   10

Beauty Parlor Bear with Lighted Dryer Stand, 1950s, S&E Co., 9½" high, seven actions
$500.00 $1,000.00   8

Beethoven – The Piano Playing Dog, a.k.a. Jolly Pianist, 1950s, Marusan Co., 8" high, five actions
$100.00 $200.00   4

Begging Puppy, 1960s, Y Co., 9" long, six actions
$40.00 $80.00   2

Bell Clanger – Silver Mountain Express, 1960s, M-T Co., 15¾" long, four actions
$40.00 $80.00   1

Bell Organ, 1957, Knickerbocker Co., 9½" long, 5½" high, minor toy, includes music book and holder
$60.00 $120.00   3

Bell Ringer Choo Choo, 1960s, M-T Co., 10" long, four actions

$30.00	$60.00	3

Bengali – The Exciting New Growling, Prowling Tiger, 1961, Marx Co., Linemar Div., 18½" long, from nose to end of tail, two cycles, three actions

$100.00	**$200.00**	**3**

Big Alarm – Giant High Rig Fire Truck, 1960s, Marx Co., 23¼" long, twelve actions, includes detachable plastic fireman, two ladders, hose, pump

$150.00	$300.00	6

Big Bruiser – Super Highway Service Tow Truck, 1960s, Marx Co., 23" long, six actions, includes tools, driver, detachable plastic boom

$150.00	$300.00	7

Big Dipper, 1960s, Technofix Co., minor toy, 21" long, 11" high, includes three tin cars

$100.00	**$200.00**	**4**

Big Hunter – Automatic Gun, 1950s, Tada Co., 21" long, extended, three actions

$50.00	$100.00	3

Big John, 1960s, Alps Co., 12" high, three actions

$60.00	$120.00	3

Big John – The Indian Chief, c.1960s, T-N Co., 12½" tall, five actions

$90.00	$180.00	4

Big Loo – Your Friend From the Moon, 1960s, Marx Co., 38" tall, twelve actions, includes balls, darts, compass, etc.

$1,000.00	$2,000.00+	9

Big Max and His Electronic Conveyor, 1958, Remco Co., 11" long, 8" high, three actions, includes 7" long, red plastic truck and 40 steel slugs

$120.00	**$240.00**	**4**

Big Circus Truck, see Circus Parade

Big Shot Cadillac, 1950s, T-N Co., 10" long, four actions

$200.00	**$400.00**	**6**

Big Top Champ Circus Clown, 1960s, Alps Co., 14" tall, three actions

$80.00	$160.00	8

Big Wheel Coca Cola Truck, 1970s, Taiyo Co., three actions
$80.00 $160.00   **3**

Big Wheel Family Camper, 1970s, Taiyo Co., 10" long, three actions
$60.00 $120.00   3

Big Wheel Ice Cream Truck, 1970s, Taiyo Co., 10" long, three actions
$60.00 $120.00   3

Biller Train No. 573, 1950s, T-N Co., 13" long, includes rubber cable track and two hopper cars, minor toy
$70.00 $140.00   3

Billy Blastoff – Space Scout, 1968, Eldon Co., 4½" tall, minor toy, includes space gun, T.V. set and space vehicles
$100.00 $200.00   6

Billy the Kid Sheriff, 1950s, Y Co., 10½" tall, two cycles, four actions
$180.00 $360.00   5

Bimbo the Drumming Clown, 1950s, Alps Co., 9¼" tall, three actions, includes detachable hat
$300.00 $600.00   6

Bingo Clown, 1950s, T-N Co., 13" tall, three actions
$200.00 $400.00   6

Bingo The Clown, 1960s, T-K-R Co., 9"-14" extended, four actions
$180.00 $360.00   9

Bird Cage Lantern, lantern toy, 1950s, A.A.A. Co. and pigeon logo, 5½" high, minor toy
$40.00 $80.00   4

Bixby and The Bunny, 1950s, Marx Co., 9½" long, (Bixby), 5½" long (Bunny), six actions
$200.00 $400.00   8

Black Knight Batmobile, unauthorized, 1960s, Alps Co., 11½" long, four actions
$250.00 $500.00   6

Blacksmith Bear, 1950s, A-1 Co., 9½" tall, six actions
$180.00 $360.00   5

Black Smithy Bear, 1950s, T-N Co., 9" high, four actions
$200.00 $400.00   7

Blink-A-Gear-Robot, 1960s, Taiyo Co., 14½" tall, five actions
$400.00 $800.00   7

Blinking Lite Submarine – Nautilus #351, 1950s, T-N Co., 10"
long, minor toy, friction drive with blinking light
$80.00 $160.00   7

Blinking Nite Lite Street Lamp, lantern toy, 1950s, G-W Co.,
6½" tall, minor toy
$60.00 $120.00   10

Blinky The Clown – With The Light In His Eyes, 1950s, Amico
Co., 10½" tall, with drum or xylophone, five actions, includes
detachable felt or paper hat
$200.00 $400.00   7

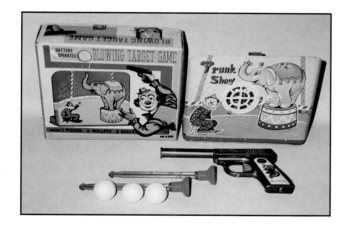

Blowing Target Game, 1950s, S-H Co., 5" high, 6" long,
minor toy, includes tin gun, darts, and styrofoam balls
$110.00 $220.00   9

Blow-Up-Ball Locomotive, 1950s, M-T Co., 9½" long, minor
toy, includes celluloid ball
$80.00 $160.00   4

Blue Comet Speedboat with Outboard Motor, 1950s, K-O
Co., 14½" long, minor toy, mostly wood
$100.00 $200.00   7

Blue Express, #4291 locomotive, 1950s, M-T Co., 11¼"
long, four actions
$40.00 $80.00   2

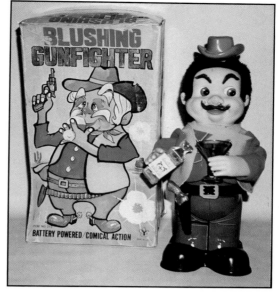

Blushing Gunfighter, 1960s, Y Co., 11" tall, five actions,
includes plastic gun
$110.00 $220.00   5

Blushing Willy, 1960s, Y Co., 10" tall, four actions
$60.00 $120.00   1

Bobby Drinking Bear, 1950s, Y Co., 10" tall, six actions
$200.00 $400.00   6

Bobby the Drumming Bear, 1950s, Alps Co., 10" tall, four
actions
$210.00 $420.00   7

Bob's Farm Tractor, 1950s, M-T Co., 9" long, three actions,
includes detachable tin driver
$90.00 $180.00   8

Boeing 727 Jet Liner, 1960s, Y Co., 17½" long, 16¼"
wingspan, three actions
$140.00 $280.00   4

Boeing 727 Jet Plane, 1960s, M-T Co., 12½" long, 10⅜" wingspan, three actions
$150.00 $300.00   4

Boeing 737 Jet Plane, 1960s, T-N Co., 12" long, 10½" wingspan
$100.00 $200.00   4

Boeing 747 Jumbo Jet Plane, Pan Am, 1960s, T-N Co., 17" long, 16" wingspan, four actions
$60.00 $120.00   3

Bombardier, 1960s, K-O Co., 10½" long, 9" wingspan, six actions
$190.00 $380.00   6

Bomber Pilot, 1960s, K-O Co., 10½" long, 9" wingspan, six actions
$190.00   **$380.00**   **5**

Bongo Monkey, 1960s, Alps Co., 9½" high, three actions, includes plastic hat
$80.00 $160.00   2

Bongo Player, 1960s, Alps Co., 10" tall, four actions
$80.00 $160.00   2

Bowling Bank, 1960s, M.B. Daniel & Co., 10" long, three actions
$90.00 $180.00   3

Brave Eagle, 1950s, T-N Co., 11" tall, five actions
$90.00 $180.00   2

Breakfast Chef, 1960s, K Co., 8¼" tall, minor toy, includes plastic egg and coffee maker
$70.00 $140.00   5

Brewster the Rooster, 1950s, Marx Co., 9½" high, five actions
$120.00 $240.00   3

Bristol 188 Jet, 1960s, Marx Co., 15" long, 9" wingspan, three actions, tin and plastic
$90.00 $180.00   4

Bristol Bulldog Airplane, T-360, S&E Co., 12" long, 14½" wingspan, lights, prop spins, stop and go, noise, four actions
$160.00 $320.00   3

Broadway Trolley, see Tinkling Trolley

Brunch Snack Bar, 1960s, K Co., 6" long, three actions, includes tin frying pan and condiments
$140.00 $280.00   6

Bruno the Accordion Bear, 1950s, Y Co., 10½" tall, five actions
$140.00   **$280.00**   **6**

Bubble Bear, 1950s, M-T Co., 9½" high, 4" x 5" base, four actions
$140.00 $280.00   4

Bubble Blowing Boil Over Car, 1950s, M-T Co., 10" long, three actions
$90.00 $180.00   3

Bubble Blowing Boy, 1950s, Y Co., 17" high, four actions
$150.00 $300.00   5

Bubble Blowing Bunny, 1950s, Y Co., 7" high, four actions
$100.00 $200.00   4

Bubble Blowing Dog, 1950s, Y Co., 8" high, three actions
$100.00 $200.00   5

Bubble Blowing Kangaroo, 1950s, M-T Co., 9" high base to tip of ears, three actions
$200.00 $400.00   7

Bubble Blowing Lion, 1950s, M-T Co., 7½" high, 3½" x 7" base, four actions
$100.00 $200.00   3

Bubble Blowing Monkey, 1950s, Alps Co., 10" tall, four actions, includes plastic bowl for bubble solution
$100.00 $200.00   2

Bubble Blowing Musician, 1950s, Y Co., 11" tall, three actions, includes plastic bowl for bubble solution
$200.00 $400.00   4

Bubble Blowing Popeye, 1950s, Linemar Co., 11¾" tall, five actions
$1,000.00 $2,000.00+   8

Bubble Blowing Washing Bear, 1950s, Y Co., 8" high, three actions, includes plastic washtub
$170.00 $340.00   6

Bubble Locomotive, 1950s, T-N Co., 9½" long, three actions
$50.00 $100.00   5

Bubbling Bull, 1950s, Linemar Co., 6½" long, 8" high, five actions, includes plastic bowl, a.k.a. Wild West Rodeo
$90.00 $180.00   4

Bubbling Pup, 1950s, Linemar Co., 7½" high, five actions
$70.00 $140.00   3

Buck Rogers Sonic Ray Gun, 1952, Norton-Honer Co., 7½" long, minor toy, includes Morse Code booklet
$150.00 $300.00   2

Bulldozer, 1950s, T-N Co., 7½" long, five actions
$60.00 $120.00   3

Bulldozer, 1950s, M-T Co., 11" long, six actions

    $70.00 $140.00   3

Bulldozer with a Robot Operator, 1960s, T-N Co., 9½" long, three actions

    $400.00 $800.00+   8

Bumping Car, bumper car, 1961, Alps Co., 10" long, minor toy

    $60.00 $120.00   7

Bunny The Cashier, 1950s, M-T Co., 7½" high, five actions

    $150.00 $300.00   5

Bunny The Magician, 1950s, Alps Co., 14½" tall, five actions, includes card-ribbon apparatus for card trick

    $250.00   **$500.00**   **6**

Burger Chef, 1950s, Y Co., 9" tall, eight actions, includes tin-litho hamburger

    $100.00   **$200.00**   **4**

Busy Bizzy Friendly Bug, 1950s, M-T Co., 6¼" long, three actions

    $60.00 $120.00   4

Busy Cart Robot, 1960s, S-H Co., 11" tall, four actions, includes plastic wheelbarrow

    $250.00 $500.00   6

Busy Housekeeper, The, bear, 1950s, Alps Co., 8½" tall, four actions

    $160.00 $320.00   5

Busy Housekeeper, The, bunny, 1950s, Alps Co., 10" tall, four actions

    $150.00 $300.00   5

Busy Secretary, 1950s, Linemar Co., 7½" high, 7¼" long, seven actions

    $150.00   **$300.00**   **5**

Busy Shoe Shining Bear, 1950s, Alps Co., 10" high, five actions

    $140.00 $280.00   4

Butt Stompin' Ashtray, 1977, Poynter Prod., 7¼" high, four actions, includes tin manhole cover, ashtray insert and 4½" high plastic shoe

    $40.00 $80.00   4

Butterfly The Flying Dog, 1960s, T-N Co., 7" long, 7" high, four actions

    $30.00 $60.00   5

Butterfly with Flapping Wings, 1950s, Linemar Co., 4" long, 10" wingspan, three actions

    $60.00   **$120.00**   **6**

Buttons – Puppy with a Brain, also called Buttons the Push
Button Pup, 1960s, Marx, 12" high, eight actions

| $200.00 | $400.00 | 5 |

Buzzer Robot, 1950s, Y Co., 11" tall, four actions, Robot
With Buzzer on box

| $1,500.00 | $3,000.00+ | 10 |

B-Z Porter Baggage Truck, 1950s, M-T Co., 7½" long, 6½"
high, minor toy, includes three pieces of luggage, tin

| $140.00 | $280.00 | 5 |

B-Z Rabbit, c.1950s, M-T Co., 7" long, four actions

| $60.00 | $120.00 | 5 |

B-Z Vendor – (Ice Cream Cart), 1950s, M-T Co., 7½" long,
three actions

| $450.00 | $900.00+ | 9 |

Cabin Cruiser, 1950s, SGK Co., 21½" long, three actions

| $150.00 | $300.00 | 6 |

Cabin Cruiser with Outboard Motor, 1950s, Linemar Co., 12"
long, minor toy

| $100.00 | $200.00 | 5 |

Cable Train, 1940s, T-N Co., 12" long, four piece set, minor
toy

| $80.00 | $160.00 | 2 |

Cadillac Car, 1949, Ashai Toy Co., 10" long, three actions

| $140.00 | $280.00 | 4 |

Calypso Joe, 1950s, Linemar, 11" tall, four actions

| $300.00 | $600.00 | 8 |

Camera Shooting Bear, A.K.A Cine Bear, 1950s, Linemar
Co., 11" tall, five actions, includes five plastic worms

| $450.00 | $900.00 | 8 |

Candy Vending Machine, bank, 1950s, W Toy Co., 9½" high,
three actions, includes tin lid and plastic funnel

| $400.00 | $800.00 | 8 |

Capitol Airlines Viscount 321, 1950s, Linemar, 11" long, 14"
wingspan, four actions

| $160.00 | $320.00 | 3 |

Cappy, the Happy Baggage Porter, 1960s, Alps Co., 12"
high, 11" long, four actions

| $100.00 | $200.00 | 4 |

Capsule-6, 1964, M-T Co., 13" long, three actions

| $150.00 | $300.00 | 8 |

Capt. Buck Flash Buzz Ray Gun, 1965, Remco Co., 9" long,
minor toy, mostly plastic

| $50.00 | $100.00 | 5 |

Captain Blushwell, 1960s, Y Co., 11" tall, six actions

| $80.00 | $160.00 | 3 |

Captain Hook, 1950s, Marusan Co., 10¾" high, three actions, includes tin sword and felt hat
  $800.00 $1,600.00+   10

Captain Kidd Pirate Ship, 1960s, Yonezawa Co., 13" long, four actions
  $200.00 $400.00   8

Captain Robo-Space Transporter in New Docking Action, 1970s, Y Co., 13½" long, assembled, two piece set
  $100.00   **$200.00**   **4**

Caterpillar, 1950s, Alps Co., 16" long, three actions
  $90.00 $180.00   5

Caterpillar Tank M-1, 1950s, M-T Co., 8½" long, 11" long, with barrel extended, five actions
  $150.00 $300.00   4

Cement Mixer, 1950s, M-T Co., 10½" long, four actions
  $110.00 $220.00   7

Central Choo Choo, 1960s, M-T Co., 15" long, three actions
  $40.00 $80.00   2

Champion Boat 2-J, 1950s, Bandai Co., 12" long, minor toy
  $120.00 $240.00   5

Champion Stunt Car, Mustang, 1960s, TPS Co., 12" long, minor toy
  $50.00 $100.00   2

Champion Weight Lifter, 1960s, Y-M Co., 10" tall, five actions
  $100.00 $200.00   2

Change Man Robot, Astronaut, 1960s, S-H Co., 13¼" tall, four actions
  $4,000.00 $8,000.00+   10

Chap – The Obedient Dog, 1960s, N Co., 10½" long, three actions
  $40.00 $80.00   2

Chaparral 2F, car, 1960s, Alps Co., 11" long, five actions
  $80.00 $160.00   3

Charlie the Drumming Clown, 1960s, Alps Co., six actions, includes detachable drum and cymbals, 9½" tall
  $150.00   **$300.00**   **3**

Charlie the Funny Clown, 1960s, Alps Co., 9" long, three actions
  $150.00 $300.00   4

Charley Weaver, 1962, T-N Co., 12" tall, six actions
  $60.00   **$120.00**   **1**

Charm the Cobra, 1960s, Alps Co., 6" high, three actions, mostly plastic
$100.00 $200.00   5

Chee Chee Chihuahua, 1960s, Mego Co., 8" high, five actions
$30.00 $60.00   2

Cheerful Dachshund, also called Cheerful Puppy Dog, 1960s, Y Co., 8½" long, five actions
$30.00 $80.00   3

Chef Cook, 1960s, Y Co., 11½" tall with hat on, five actions, includes tin litho egg and hat
$150.00 $300.00   3

Chemical Fire Engine, 1950s, HTC Co., 10" long, four actions
$100.00 $200.00   5

Chief Big Mouth Target Game, 1950s, Marx Co., 13" high, minor toy, includes gun, plastic darts, styrofoam balls
$150.00 $300.00   8

Chief Robotman, 1950s, K.O. Co., 12" tall, four actions
$450.00 $900.00   6

Chief Smoky—Advanced Robotman, 1950s, K-O Co., Yoshia, 12" tall, five actions
$1,500.00 $3,000.00+   10

Chiefy The Fire Dog, 1969, Alps Co., 9" long, three actions, includes plastic fireman's hat
$50.00 $100.00   5

Children Island, 1950s, M-T Co., 19" long, minor toy similar to Space Trip, includes two tin cars
$400.00 $800.00   10

Chimp and Pup Rail Car, 1950s, T-N Co., 8" high, four actions
$90.00 $180.00   4

Chimp With Xylophone, 1970s, Y Co., 12" long, 8" high, minor toy, includes four records and hammer
$100.00 $200.00   8

Chimpy the Jolly Drummer, 1950s, Alps Co., 9" high, six actions, includes detachable drum and cymbals
$70.00 $140.00   3

Chippy the Chipmunk, 1950s, Alps Co., 12" long, nosetip to tail tip, four actions
$90.00 $180.00   3

Chirping Grasshopper, 1950s, M-T Co., 8½" long, three actions
$90.00 $180.00   5

Chirri-Biplane, 1950s, Rico Co., Spain, 10" long, 11½" wingspan, four actions
$150.00 $300.00   3

Chris Craft Motor Boat, 1950s, I.T.O. Co., 12" long, minor toy, mostly wood
$150.00 $300.00   6

Christmas Time, 1950s, Murusan Co., 10" high, 7" base diameter, three actions
$500.00 $1,000.00+   10

Chuckling Charlie—The Hysterical Laughing Clown, 1960s, S-H Co., six actions, similar to The Laughing Clown
$150.00 $300.00   6

Cindy the Meowing Cat, 1950s, Tomiyama Co., 12" high nosetip to tail tip, two cycles, four actions
$50.00 $100.00   4

Cine Bear, see Camera Shooting Bear.

Circular Saw, 1950s, T-N Co., 7" long, 5" high, minor toy
$20.00 $40.00   6

Circus Elephant, 1960s, Yanoman Co., 9" long, four actions
$40.00 $80.00   3

Circus Elephant with Blowing Ball and Parasol, 1950s, T-N Co., 9¾" high, three actions, includes celluloid ball and tin umbrella
$150.00 $300.00   3

Circus Fire Engine, 1960s, M-T Co., 11" long, four actions
    $130.00   **$260.00**   **6**

Circus Jet, T-N Co., 9" high assembled, Jet 6¼" long, three actions
    $90.00 $180.00   4

Circus Lion, 1950s, Rock Valley Toy Co., Via., 11" high, four actions, includes whip and flannel carpet with levers, two cycles
    $300.00 $600.00   8

Circus Parade, 1950s, M-T Co., 13" long, three actions
    $190.00   **$380.00**   **5**

Clancy the Great, 1960s, Ideal Toy Co., three actions, 19½" tall without hat, includes plastic hat and test coin
    $100.00 $200.00   2

Clang Clang Locomotive, 1950s, Marx Co., Japan: M-T Co., 10½" long, three actions
    $30.00 $60.00   3

Climbing Donald Duck On His Friction Fire Engine, 1950s, Linemar Co., 18" long, truck, 5½" tall Donald Duck
    $600.00 $1,200.00+   9

Climbing Fireman, 1950s, TPS Co., 24" high assembled, five actions, includes three tin ladder sections
    $200.00 $400.00   8

Climbing Linesman, 1950s, TPS Co., 24" high when assembled, three actions, includes three tin pole sections
    $300.00 $600.00   8

Clown Circus Car, 1960s, M-T Co., 8½" long, 9" high, five actions
    $140.00 $280.00   5

Clown and Lion, 1960s, M-T Co., 11¾" high from base to top of tree, four actions
    $240.00   480.00   6

Clown on Unicycle, 1960s, M-T Co., 10½" high, three actions
    $210.00 $420.00   7

Clown's Bank, The, 1940s, unmarked, 10" high, minor toy, all plastic
    $80.00 $160.00   4

Clown's Popcorn Truck, 1960s, TPS Co., 6" long, five actions, mostly plastic
    $140.00   **$280.00**   **7**

Clown-The-Magician, No. 40244, 1950s, Alps Co., 12" tall, six actions, includes card-ribbon apparatus for card trick
    $200.00 $400.00   4

Coast Guards with Flag Waving Action, 1950s, Y Co., 8½" long, minor toy
    $90.00 $180.00   8

Coca-Cola Dispenser – Bank, 1950s, Linemar Co., minor toy, 9½" tall, includes four plastic Coke glasses and rubber stopper

$450.00	**$900.00**	**6**

Coca-Cola Route Truck, 1950s, Sanyo Co., 12" long, minor toy

$170.00	$340.00	6

Cock-A-Doodle-Doo Rooster, 1950s, Mikuni Co., 8" high, four actions

$80.00	**$160.00**	**5**

Coffeetime Bear, 1960s, T-N Co., 10" tall, five actions, similar to Maxwell Coffee-Loving Bear

$120.00	$240.00	2

Coin Operated Battery Cab, 1950s, Kanto Co., 9" long, minor toy

$200.00	$400.00	8

Coin Taxi, 1970s, Daiya Co., 6½" long, minor toy, bank

$60.00	$120.00	3

Collie, 1950s, Alps Co., 9" long, five actions

$40.00	$80.00	5

Colonel Hap Hazard, Robot, 1968, Marx Co., 11¼" tall, four actions, includes lighted bar antenna

$350.00	$700.00	6

Combat G.I., 1960s, Linemar Co., 10" long, four actions, uses roll caps

$100.00	$200.00	7

Combi-O-Mixer, 1950s, Excelo Co., mixer-blender, 9" long, 9" high, minor toy

$30.00	$60.00	4

Comic Choo Choo, 1960s, Cragstan Co., 10¼" long, three actions

$40.00	$80.00	3

Comic Hungry Bug, VW auto, 1970s, Tora S-T Co., 7¾" long, five actions

$40.00	$80.00	3

Comic Musical Car, 1960s, T-N Co., 6" long, 8½" tall, four actions

$70.00	$140.00	4

Comic Road Grader, 1950s, Bandai Co., 9" long, four actions

$70.00	$140.00	3

Comic Road Roller, 1960s, Bandai Co., 9" long, four actions

$70.00	$140.00	3

Communication Truck, 1950s, M-T Co., 12" long, minor toy, friction powered and B.O. lights

$70.00	$140.00	6

Coney Island Penny Machine, 1950s, Remco Co., 13" high, minor toy, includes plastic prizes

$120.00	**$240.00**	**4**

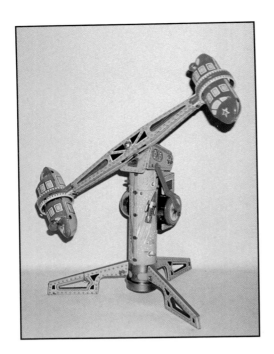

Coney Island Rocket Ride, 1950s, Alps Co., 13½" high, four actions, same as Twirly-Whirly

$400.00 $800.00   **6**

Continental Blue Locomotive, 1960s, M-T Co., 12½" long, four actions

$30.00 $60.00   2

Continental Flyer Train Set, 1960s, Y Co., 21" long, assembled, four actions, twelve piece set

$30.00 $90.00   4

Conveyancer Fork Track, 1950s, Owen Co., England, 10" long, extended, three actions, includes mosel loads, pallets, and crane attachment

$150.00 $300.00   8

Corvair Bertone, 1970s, Bandai Co., 12" long, four actions

$50.00 $100.00   3

Corvette, '68 Chevy, 1968, Taiyo Co., 10" long, minor toy

$60.00 $120.00   **3**

Corvette Stingray Sport Coupe, 1968, Eldon Co., 13½" long, minor toy

$60.00 $120.00   2

Cowboy Riding Horse, 1950s, T-N Co., 7" high, three actions

$70.00 $140.00   5

Cragstan Air Defense Center Missile Launcher, 1960s, Cragstan Co., 7½" long, six actions, includes three plastic darts and antenna

$200.00 $400.00   6

Cragstan Astronaut, Daiya Co., 14" tall, four actions, blue or red

$400.00 $800.00   **4**

Cragstan Beep Beep Greyhound Bus, 1950s, Cragstan Co., 20" long, three actions

$110.00 $220.00   5

Cragstan Biplane, 7F7, U.S. Navy, 1950s, T-N Co., 9½" long, 11½" wingspan, four actions

$200.00 $400.00   6

Cragstan Biplane, 7F18, 1950s, T-N Co., 12" long, 14⅜" wingspan, five actions

$220.00 $440.00   6

Cragstan Cap Firing Gunboat, U.S.S. Faragut, 1960s, NGS Co., 15½" long, four actions

$150.00 $300.00   5

Cragstan Crapshooter, 1950s, Y Co., 9½" tall, four actions, includes pair of small dice

$100.00 $200.00   1

Cragstan Crapshooting Monkey, 1950s, Alps Co., 9" tall, three actions, includes pair of small dice

$90.00 $180.00   2

Cragstan Dog Shuttling Train Set, 1960s, Y Co., 38" long, extended, four actions, includes tin sugar barrel

$90.00 $180.00   5

Cragstan Firebird III, 1950s, Alps Co., 11½" long, three actions

$250.00   **$500.00**   **3**

Cragstan Flying Plane With Pylon Tower, 1950s, Cragstan Co., plane 8" long, 9½" wingspan, tower 26" high, minor toy

$120.00 $240.00   6

Cragstan Great Astronaut, 1960s, Alps Co., 14" tall, five actions

$500.00 $1,000.00+   9

Cragstan Jumping Princess Poodle, 1950s, NGS Co., 9" long, 8" high, five actions

$40.00 $80.00   2

Cragstan Mister Robot, 1960s, Cragstan Co., 11" tall, three actions, mostly plastic

$190.00 $380.00   8

Cragstan's Mr. Robot, 1960s, Y Co., 10½" tall, four actions

$350.00   **$700.00**   **6**

Cragstan Mother Goose, 1960s, Y Co., 8¼" high, six actions

$90.00 $180.00   5

Cragstan Multi-Action DC-7C Plane, 1950s, Y Co., 21½" long, 23½" wingspan, five actions with sequential spinning propellors

$350.00 $700.00   6

Cragstan Mystery Action Satellite with Astronaut in Orbit, a.k.a. Satellite X-107, 1960s, Alps, M-T Co., 9" dia., four actions

$500.00 $1,000.00   8

Cragstan One-Arm Bandit, 1960s, Y Co., 6¼" high, three actions, includes 3" x 3¼" sign

$100.00   **$200.00**   **6**

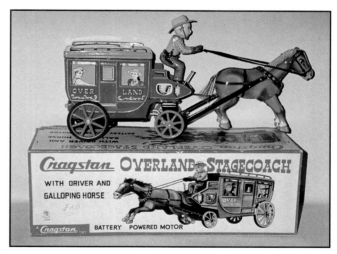

Cragstan Overland Stage Coach, 1960s, Ichida Co., 18" long, four actions

$100.00   **$200.00**   **2**

Cragstan Playboy, 1960s, Cragstan Co., 13" high, five actions

$100.00 $200.00   4

Cragstan Ranger Robot, 1960s, Cragstan Co., 10½" tall, five actions, mostly plastic

$500.00 $1,000.00+   9

Cragstan Remote Control Jeep—#10560, 1950s, Cragstan Co., 7" long, minor toy

$40.00 $80.00   6

Cragstan Rolling Honey Bear, 1950s, Y Co., 7½" tall, minor toy

$40.00 $80.00   4

Cragstan Roulette – A Gambling Man, 1960s, Y Co., 9" tall, five actions, includes steel ball, chips, tin table, game sheet

$140.00 $280.00   4

Cragstan Satellite, 1950s, Cragstan Co., 8" diameter, 5½" high

$90.00 $180.00   3

Cragstan Smoking Jet Plane—U.S.A.F., see Jet Plane with Smoking & Tail Light

Cragstan Space—Mobile, 1960s, Cragstan Co., 11" long, five actions, includes detachable plastic antenna

$250.00 $500.00   8

Cragstan Talking Robot, 1960s, Y Co., 10½" tall, three actions

$360.00 $720.00   6

Cragstan Telly Bear, 1950s, S&E Co., 8" high, six actions
$240.00 $480.00   4

Cragstan Tootin'-Chuggin' Locomotive, 1950s, Cragstan Co., 24" long, three actions, longest single piece battery toy made

$70.00 $140.00   5

Cragstan Tugboat, 1950s, San Co., 12¾" long, three actions

$140.00 $280.00   4

Cragstan Vertol 1107 Helicopter, 1950s, T-N Co., 13½" long, four actions includes rotors

$120.00 $240.00   4

Cragstan Western Locomotive, 1950s, Cragstan Co., 12" long, four actions

$60.00 $120.00   2

Cragstan's Two Gun Sheriff, 1950s, Y Co., 9½" tall, five actions, includes tin hat

$130.00 $260.00   3

Crane Tractor, 1950s, SKK Co., 7½" long, 11½" high extended

$70.00 $140.00   3

Crawling Baby, 1940s, Linemar Co., 11" long, 8½" high, minor toy

$50.00 $100.00   3

Crazy Car, 1950s, Marusan Co., 9" long, five actions
$60.00 $120.00   4

Crazy Express, 1960s, Marx Co., 17" long, minor toy

$50.00 $100.00   2

Cross Country Express, 1950s, K Co., 13" long, minor toy

$50.00 $100.00   3

Crown Winker Light House, lantern toy, 1950s, Crown Electric Works, Ltd., 5" high, minor toy

$30.00 $60.00   3

Cute Poodle, 1950s, Y Co., 10" high, 8" long, six actions

$30.00 $60.00   2

Cuty Cook, elephant or hippo, 1960s, Y Co., 9½" tall, five actions, includes chef hat and tin litho egg
$150.00 $300.00+   8

Cycling Daddy, 1960s, Bandai Co., 10" high, four actions
$110.00 $220.00   3

Cyclist Clown, 1950s, K Co., 7" high, seven actions
$200.00 $400.00   6

Cyclist Clown, 1950s, M-T Co., 6½" high, six actions
$200.00 $400.00   6

Cyclist Clown, 1950s, Alps Co., 9" high, five actions
$200.00 $400.00   6

Cyclist Penguin, 1950s, K Co., 6½" high, six actions
$210.00 $420.00   8

Cymbal Playing Turnover Monkey, 1960s, T-N Co., 8" tall, three actions
$50.00 $100.00   3

Dachshund, 1950s, Y Co., 9" long, five actions
$50.00 $100.00   4

Daisy The Jolly Drumming Duck, 1950s, Alps Co., 9" high, seven actions, includes detachable drum and cymbals
$140.00 $280.00   5

Dalmatian One-Man Band No. 90262, 1950s, Alps Co., 9" high, six actions, includes detachable cymbals and drum
$120.00 $240.00   4

Dancing Dan with His Mystery Mike, 1950s, Bell Prod. Co., 13½" tall, minor toy
$100.00 $200.00   5

Dancing Merry Chimp, 1960s, Kuramochi Co., C-K, 11" tall, five actions
$100.00 $200.00   3

Dancing Nicky The Clown Lantern, lantern toy, 1950s, Marbo Co., 6" long, minor toy
$50.00 $100.00   5

Dancing Santa Lantern, lantern toy, 1950s, Marbo Co., 5½" long, minor toy
$20.00 $40.00   2

Dancing Sweethearts, 1950s, T-N Co., 7" tall, minor toy
$90.00 $180.00   4

Dandy The Happy Drumming Pup, 1950s, Alps Co., 8½" high, includes detachable drum and cymbals
$110.00 $220.00   4

Daredevil Stunt Motorcyclist, 1950s, T-N Co., 10½" long, four actions
$200.00 $400.00   6

Dashee The Derby Hat Dachshund, 1971, Mego Corp., 8" long, four actions, includes plastic derby
$40.00 $80.00   6

Dennis the Menace (Playing London Bridge), 1950s, Rosko, 9" high, three actions, includes xylophone

$150.00	**$300.00**	**6**

Dentist Bear, 1950s, S&E Co., 9½" tall, 6¾"x4¼" base, seven actions, includes detachable head

$300.00	$600.00	5

Desert Patrol Jeep, 1960s, M-T Co., 11" long, four actions, includes turret gunner

$90.00	$180.00	3

Destroyer 206, 1950s, Y Co., 14" long, six actions, includes seven depth charges

$110.00	**$220.00**	**4**

Dick Tracy Police Car, 1949, Linemar Co., 9" long, four actions

$200.00	$400.00	3

Diesel Locomotive, 1950s, Cragstan Co., minor toy, 16½" long

$30.00	$60.00	2

Dilly Dalmatian, 1950s, Cragstan Co., 9½" long, five actions

$60.00	$120.00	7

Dino Robot, 1960s, S-H Co., 11" tall, five actions

$500.00	$1,000.00+	8

Dip-ie the Whale, 1960s, S-H Co., 13" long tall, three actions

$250.00	$500.00	6

Directional Robot, see Robot

Dish Washer-Automatic, 1950s, Alps Co., 9" high, minor toy, includes 24 piece utensil set, two dish baskets, tin tray

$60.00	**$120.00**	**3**

Disney Acrobats, Mickey, Donald & Pluto, 1950s, Linemar Co., 9" high, minor toy

$500.00	$1,000.00+	8

Disney Fire Engine, 1950s, Linemar Co., 11" long, four actions

$440.00	$880.00	8

Disney Piston Race Car, Mickey Mouse, 1960s, M-T Co., 9¾" long, four actions

$80.00	$160.00	5

Disneyland Fire Engine, 1950s, Linemar Co., 18" long, five actions

$350.00	$700.00	8

Diving Submarine, Nautilus, 1950s, 12" long, minor toy

$90.00	$180.00	5

Doak-16 VTOL Airplane, 1950s, Alps Co., 15" long, 13" wingspan, five actions

$250.00	$500.00	5

Docking Rocket, 1960s, Daiya Co., 16" long, 24" extended, six actions, includes plastic radar antenna

$100.00	$200.00	6

Dr. Who—The Mysterious Daleks, from the BBC television series, 1970s, Hong Kong, 7" high, minor toy, mostly plastic

$90.00	$180.00	2

Dodge-Em Tricky Action Game, 1970s, Cragstan Co., 5" long, minor toy, includes two cars

$60.00	$120.00	4

Dog Family, 1960s, Alps Co., 1" long, four actions
$30.00 $60.00   2

Dog Shuttling Train Set, 1950s, Y Co., 38" long extended, with 6" long tin R.R. car, four actions, includes two barrels of sugar
$200.00 $400.00   7

Dog Sled, 1950s, T-N Co., 14" long, four actions
$300.00 $600.00   6

Dolly Dressmaker, 1950s, T-N Co., 7" high, ten actions, includes cloth sample, Dolly Seamstress on box
$150.00 $300.00   3

Dolly Seamstress, see Dolly Dressmaker

Donald Duck, 1960s, Linemar Co., 8" tall, four actions
$200.00 $400.00   7

Donald Duck Locomotive, 1970s, M-T Co., six actions, 9" long
$150.00 $300.00   5

Donald Duck Trolley, 1960s, M-T Co., 11" high, three actions
$160.00 $320.00   6

Donny the Smiling Bulldog, 1961, Tomiyama Co., 8½" long, three actions, two cycles
$75.00 $150.00   5

Door Robot, see Robot, Revolving and Flashing

Douglas C-124 Globe Master, 1950s, Yonezawa Co., 20½" wingspan, 18" long, eight actions
$300.00 $600.00   6

Douglas DC-9TWA Jet Plane, 1960s, T-N Co., 14" long, 17" wingspan, four actions
$100.00 $200.00   4

Doxie the Dog, 1950s, Linemar Co., 9" long, five actions
$30.00 $60.00   3

Dozzo-the-Steaming Clown, 1960s, T-N Co., Rosko toys, 10" tall, five actions
$200.00 $400.00   3

Dragon Speed Boat, 1950s, T-M-Y Co., 18" long, minor toy
$400.00 $800.00   8

Dream Boat Hot Rod, see Hot Rod

Drill, 1950s, Linemar Co., 6" long, includes attachments, minor toy
$20.00 $40.00   3

Drinker's Savings Bank, 1960s, Illfelder Co., 9" high, minor toy
$90.00 $180.00   2

Drinking Bear, 1970s, Alps Co., 12" high, six actions
$60.00 $120.00   5

Drinking Captain, 1960s, S&E Co., 12" tall, six actions
$100.00 $200.00   2

Drinking Dog, 1950s, with lighted eyes, Y Co., 7" high, four actions
$90.00 $180.00   4

Drinking Dog With Lighted Eyes, 1950s, Y Co., 9" high, four actions

$90.00 $180.00   4

Drinking—Licking Cat, 1950s, T-N Co., 10" high, 4"x4" base, six actions

$120.00 $240.00   5

Drinking Monkey, 1950s, Alps Co., 10" high, five actions

$100.00 $200.00   5

Drum Bear, c.1950s, Alps Co., 7¾" tall, five actions

$100.00 $200.00   6

Drum Monkey, 1970s, Yada Co., 8" high, three actions

$40.00 $80.00   3

Drummer Bear, 1950s, Alps Co., 10" tall, six actions

$140.00 $280.00   4

Drumming Bear, 1960s, Alps Co., 11½" tall, four actions
$30.00   **$60.00**   **4**

Drumming Mickey Mouse, 1950s, Linemar, 10" tall, four actions

$700.00 $1,400.00+   7

Drumming Polar Bear, 1960s, Alps Co., 12" tall, three actions

$100.00 $200.00   6

Dual-Lite Marine Speedster, (speedboat), 1950s, G. W. Co., 12" long, minor toy, mostly wood

$60.00 $120.00   6

Duck Shooting Target Game, 1950s, Linemar Co., 10" diameter, three actions, includes gun and darts

$50.00 $100.00   6

Duck with Moving Butterfly on Tail and Voice, 1950s, Marx Co., 4" long, 4 actions

$120.00 $240.00   6

Ducky Duckling, 1960s, Alps Co., 8" high, four actions

$50.00 $100.00   5

Dump Tractor, truck, 1950s, T-N Co., 8" long, three actions

$60.00 $120.00   5

Dump Truck No. 7343, 1960s, T-N Co., 10¼" long, seven actions

$60.00 $120.00   5

Dune Buggy, 1960s, TPS Co., 11" long, three actions, mostly plastic

$50.00 $100.00   4

Dune Buggy, 1960s, Alps Co., 9½" long, minor toy

$60.00 $120.00   4

Dune Buggy, 1970s, Bandai Co., 9½" long, three actions

$40.00 $80.00   4

Dynamic Fighter Robot, 1960s, Junior Toy Co., 10" tall, five actions
$70.00   **$140.00**   **5**

Early Model Limousine, 1960s, Alps Co., 9½" long, five actions

$70.00 $140.00   5

Earth Satellite, 1950s, Alps Co., 7½" long control with 2½" diameter satellite, minor toy

$200.00 $400.00   8

Earthman—Astronaut, 1950s, T-N Co., 9½" tall, five actions
$900.00 $1,800.00+   8

Electra-Matic '50' pistol, 1950s, Hubley Co., 7½" long, minor toy
$60.00 $120.00   6

Electric Convertible, 1950s, Marx Co., 20" long, minor toy
$150.00 $300.00   7

Electric Lucky Car, 1950s, M-T Co., 7" long, three actions
$200.00 $400.00   6

Electric Model Boat, 1950s, Lang Craft Co., 11" long, minor toy
$60.00 $120.00   6

Electric Powered TV and Radio Station, 1950s, Marx, 30" long, three actions
$80.00 $160.00   5

Electric Remote Control Robot, 1950s, M-T Co., 7½" tall, four actions
$500.00 $1,000.00   8

Electric Robot, 1950s, Marx, 14½" tall, five actions, no son
$100.00 $200.00   2

Electric Robot, 1950s, Marx, 14½" tall, five actions, with son
$150.00 $300.00   3

Electric School Bus, 1950s, M-T Co., 9½" long, minor toy
$70.00 $140.00   5

Electric Train Set, Rock Island Line, 1950s, M Co., minor toy, three piece set, ten track sections and track crossing
$75.00 $150.00   6

Electric Train Set—HO Gauge, 1950s, MRK Co., 17" long assembled, minor toy
$100.00 $200.00   6

Electro Radiant #5600—KLM—The Flying Dutchman, 1950s, Schuco Co., Germany, 16½" long, 19" wingspan, seven actions, sequential spinning propellers
$450.00 $900.00   8

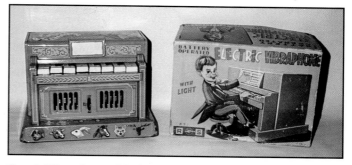

Electric Vibraphone, 1950s, T-N Co., 7½" l, 5½" h, three actions
$70.00 $140.00   4

Electro Special Racer, 1950s, Yonezawa Co., 10" long, three actions
$500.00 $1,000.00   7

Electrotoy Sand Loader, 1950s, T-N Co., 10½" long, four actions
$80.00 $160.00   5

Electro Submarino, 1950s, Schuco Co., 12" long, minor toy
$125.00 $250.00   5

Electro Train Transcontinental, 1950s, M Co., 20½" long, three pieces, three actions
$90.00 $180.00   4

Electronic Countdown, 1959, Ideal Toy Co., 24" long, six actions
$60.00 $120.00   5

Electronic Fighter Jet 4800, 1950s, Ideal Toy Co., 19" l, 11 actions
$120.00 $240.00   6

Electronic Fire House, 1940s, Banner Co., 7" square, minor toy, includes plastic fire engine
$70.00 $140.00   7

Electronic Periscope (Nautilus) Firing Range, 1950s, Cragstan, 11" high on tripod, three actions
$100.00 $200.00   5

Electronic Twin–Train Set #372, 1950s, Woodhaven Metal Stamping Co., minor toy, 28" long, 11" wide, includes two three piece trains

    $100.00 $200.00   4

El Toro–The Fighting, Snorting Bull And The Matador, 1950s, T-N Co., 9½" long assembled, four actions, includes detachable tin matador

    $125.00   **$250.00**   **7**

End Loader, 1950s, KKK Co., 8" long, three actions

    $90.00 $180.00   6

Engine Robot, 1960s, S-H Co., 9½" tall, four actions

    $100.00 $200.00   4

Esso Tiger, see Walking Tiger

Excalibur, car, 1960s, Bandai Co., 10" long, three actions

    $80.00 $160.00   6

Excavator Robot, 1960s, S-H Co., 10" tall, four actions

    $100.00   **$200.00**   **3**

Expert Motor Cyclist, 1950s, M-T Co., 12" long, five actions, a.k.a. Atom Motorcycle

    $600.00 $1,200.00   7

Explo-Robotron–The Mechanical Maniac, 1970s, Topper Corp., Japan, 6½" tall, three actions

    $70.00 $140.00   5

Exploration Train, 1950s, K Co., 24" long assembled, minor toy, includes locomotive, three cars, tracks, shells, missiles, etc.

    $400.00 $800.00   8

Explorer–Vanguard Tracking Station #801, 1960s, Structo Toy Co., 9½" long, five actions, with detachable antenna and tower

    $110.00 $220.00   7

F-14-A Navy Jet Fighter, 1960s, T-N Co., 13" long, 13" wingspan, six actions

    $200.00 $400.00   5

F-101A Voodoo Fighter, 1960s, K-O Co., 15" long, 14" wingspan, minor toy

    $100.00 $200.00   4

F-105 Thunderchief Jet Fighter, 1960s, Y Co., 17" long, 15" wingspan, five actions

    $150.00 $300.00   5

FA-059–Fighter Plane, jet with prop, 1950s, T-N Co., 11" long, 13" wingspan, five actions

    $170.00 $340.00   4

F.D. Fire Engine, 1950s, Y Co., 9¼" long, three actions

    $60.00 $120.00   8

Fairyland Loco, locomotive, 1950s, Daiya Co., 9" long, four actions

    $60.00 $120.00   5

Farm Truck, 1960s, Alps Co., 11" long, three actions

    $120.00   **$240.00**   **3**

Farm Truck, 1950s, T-N Co., 9" long, five actions
$120.00 $240.00   2

Father Bear Reading And Drinking In His Old Rocking Chair, 1950s, M-T Co., 9½" high, four actions
$175.00   **$350.00**   **8**

F.B.I. Godfather Car, 1970s, Bandai Co., 10" long, three actions
$40.00 $80.00   4

F.D. Fire Engine, 1960s, Y-M Co., 10" long, 12" high when ladder is extended, four actions
$110.00 $220.00   4

Feeding Bird Watcher, 1950s, Linemar, 9" high, five actions, includes detachable tin branch and bird
$300.00   **$600.00**   **6**

Ferrari Gear Shift Car, 1950s, Bandai Co., 11" long, three actions
$180.00 $360.00   4

Ferris Wheel Truck, c.1950s, Linemar Co., 11" long, four actions
$400.00 $800.00   7

Ferris Wheel Truck, ball blowing toy, 1960s, TPS Co., 6" long, 7" high, four actions, mostly plastic, includes styrofoam ball
$70.00 $140.00   6

Fido—The Xylophone Player, c.1950s, Alps Co., 8¾" high, body sways, head turns, arms activate lights, sound, six actions, includes detachable xylophone
$125.00   **$250.00**   **8**

Fighter (Airplane), 1960s, K-O Co., 10½" long, 9" wingspan, six actions
$160.00 $320.00   6

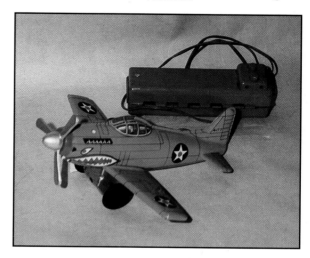

Fighter Airplane, c.1960s, Marx Co., 7" wingspan, four actions
$60.00   **$120.00**   **2**

Fighter Jet, c.1960s, Marx Co., 7" wingspan, four actions
$60.00 $120.00   2

Fighting Bull, 1960s, Alps Co., 9½" long, five actions
$70.00 $140.00   4

Fighting Bull, 1970s, Rock Valley Tech Co., 12" long, nose to tail tip, four actions, two cycles
$100.00 $200.00   4

Fighting L.S.T., 1950s, Marx Co., 18" long, multi-automatic and manual actions, includes detachable plastic antenna and missiles
$300.00 $600.00   9

Fighting Robot, 1970s, S-H Co., 10" tall, all plastic, four actions
$70.00 $140.00   4

Fighting Spaceman, 1960s, S-H Co., 12" tall, five actions
$150.00 $300.00   4

Fire Bird #7, 1950s, S–S–N Co., 12" long, three actions
$150.00 $300.00   8

Firebired '99' Dashmobile, 1960s, Remco Co., 13" long, 10" high, four actions
$110.00 $220.00   6

Firebird Racer, 1950s, Tomiyama Co., 14¼" long, four actions
$300.00 $600.00   6

Fire Boat, 1950s, M-T Co., 15" long, five actions
$150.00 $300.00   6

Fire Chief Car, '56 Buick, 1950s, Cragstan Co., 7" long, four actions
$80.00 $160.00   4

Fire Chief Car, '56 Chevy, 1950s, Linemar Co., 7" long, four actions
$80.00 $160.00   4

Fire Chief Emergency Car, '54 Chevy, 1950s, Linemar Co., 9" long, four actions
$80.00 $160.00   5

Fire Chief Mystery Action Car, 1960s, T-N Co., 9¾" long, four actions
$130.00 $260.00   5

Fire Chief No. 8 Car, 1960s, Y Co., 11¼" long, three actions
$90.00 $180.00   4

Fire Command Car, 1950s, T-N Co., five actions
$170.00 $340.00   5

Fire Dept. Jeep, 1950s, Daiya Co., 9½" long, four actions
$110.00 $220.00   6

Fire Engine, 1950s, Marusan Co., 9" long, four actions
$120.00 $240.00   4

Fire Engine, 1950s, T-N Co., Electro Toy, 9" long, ladder extends 13", three actions
$150.00 $300.00   4

Fire Engine, 1950s, Y Co., 12" long, ladder extends 16", six actions
$100.00 $200.00   5

Fire Engine, c.1950s, S-H Co., 8" long, three actions
$100.00 $200.00   4

Fire Engine, 1960s, S-H Co., 13½" long, four actions
$80.00 $160.00   5

Fire Patrol Boat, 1950s, KKS Co., 12" long, three actions
$110.00 $220.00   5

Fire Tricycle, 1950s, T-N Co., 9½" long, four actions
$180.00 $360.00   5

Firefly Bug, 1950s, T-N Co., 9" long, three actions
$100.00 $200.00   2

Firefly Racer #1, 1950s, Mormac Co., Cleveland, Ohio, 10¼" long, minor toy
$200.00 $400.00   5

Fishing Bear, 1950s, Alps Co., 10" high, six actions includes detachable pond, tin fish and hat

$140.00	**$280.00**	**3**

Fishing Bears—Bank, 1950s, Wonderful Toy Co., 9½" high, six actions

$500.00	$1,000.00+	10

Fishing Panda Bear, 1950s, Alps Co., 10" high, six actions, includes detachable pond, tin fish and hat

$150.00	**$300.00**	**4**

Fishing Polar Bear, 1950s, Alps Co., 10" high, six actions, includes detachable pond, tin fish and hat

$160.00	$320.00	5

Flag Fire Engine, 1970s, M-T Co., 9½" long, five actions

$70.00	$140.00	5

Flapping Ears Bubbling Pup, 1950s, Linemar Co., 8" high, three actions, includes plastic bowl

$60.00	$120.00	8

Flash Space Patrol—Z-206, 1960s, TPS Co., 8" long, four actions, includes detachable three bladed plastic rotor

$140.00	$280.00	6

Flashing Jet—FC-657 Airplane—U.S.A.F. 7452, 1950s, Marx Co., 7" long, 6" wingspan, four actions

$100.00	$200.00	6

Flashing Rocket Ship Space Pistol, 1950s, Irwin Co., 7½" long, four actions, mostly plastic

$40.00	$80.00	6

Flashy Flickers Magic Picture Gun, 1950s, Marx Co., 16" long, minor toy, includes five film strips

$50.00	$100.00	3

Flashy Jim, 1950s, S.N.K. Co., Ace, 7¾" tall, minor toy

$1,000.00	**$2,000.00+**	**9**

Flashy Ray Space Gun, 1950s, T-N Co., 18½" long, minor toy

$50.00	$100.00	5

Flexie The Pocket Monkey, 1960s, Alps Co., 12" tall, three actions

$75.00	$150.00	6

Flintstone Paddy Wagon, 1960s, Remco Co., 18" long, minor toy, mostly plastic

$70.00	$140.00	4

Flintstone Yacht, 1961, Remco Co., 17" l, minor toy, mostly plastic

$100.00	$200.00	3

Flippy—The Only Roller Skating Monkey That Skis, 1950s, Alps Co., 12" tall, three actions, includes tin skis

$140.00	$280.00	8

Floating Satellite Target Game, 1960s, S-H Co., 8½" high, includes tin gun, rubber tipped darts, and celluloid ball

$100.00	$200.00	2

Florida Air Boat, 1950s, ATC Co., 8" long, minor toy

    $150.00 $300.00   6

Flutter Birds, 1950s, Alps Co., 26½" high when assembled, six actions, includes detachable pulley assembly

    $300.00 $600.00   8

Flying Circus, 1960s, Tomiyama Co., 17" high assembled, three actions, includes "circus" box, "Flyer" Bear, and net

    $500.00 $1,000.00   8

Flying Dutchman—PH-KLM Airliner, 1950s, T-N Co., 11" long, 14" wingspan, five actions

    $100.00 $200.00   6

Flying Jet Plane—Boeing 747P, 1960s, J Toy Co., 13" long, 12" wingspan, five actions

    $90.00 $180.00   5

Flying Platform, 1950s, Cragstan Co., four actions, 5½" diameter, 9" high, includes detachable tin soldier

    $200.00 $400.00   8

Flying Saucer, 1970s, Y Co., 9" diameter, four actions, includes detachable antenna

    $90.00 $180.00   4

Flying Saucer—Moon Patrol 11, 1960s, Y Co., 9" dia., four actions

    $100.00   **$200.00**   **6**

Flying Saucer With Space Pilot, 1950s, K–O Co., 7½" diameter, five actions, includes conical spring antenna

    $100.00 $200.00   3

Flying Space Saucer, 1960s, A.S.C. Co., 9" diameter, three actions, includes two plastic missiles

    $300.00 $600.00   9

Flying Tiger Airplane, 1960s, Marx Co., 7" long, 7" wingspan, four actions, remote control

    $60.00 $120.00   5

Flying Tiger Line Airliner, see Swing Tail Cargo Plane—Flying Tiger

Fontainbleau #763–380, boat, 1950s, Schuco Co., 22" long, four actions, mostly plastic

    $60.00 $120.00   6

Ford 4000 HD Forklift, 1950s, Alps Co., 11½" long, extended, 9" long folded, five actions, includes tin pallet, crate, detachable canopy and driver

    $140.00 $280.00   9

Ford Fairlane, 1955, Ichida Ca, 8" long, minor toy

    $60.00 $120.00   7

Ford Gyron, 1960s, Ichida Co., 11" long, three actions

    $250.00 $500.00   7

Ford Model T, 1950s, Nihonkogei Co., 10¼" long, four actions, includes detachable tin roof

    $60.00 $120.00   5

Ford Mustang, New Duet Action, 1960s, Taiyo Co., 10" long, three actions

    $60.00 $120.00   1

Ford Mustang 2"x2", 1960s, Wenmac–AMF Co., 16" long, four actions

    $60.00 $120.00   3

Ford Skyliner, 1950s, T-N Co., 9" long, four actions

    $100.00 $200.00   4

Ford Thunderbird Convertible With Opening Door, 1960s, Bandai Co., 11" long, four actions

    $100.00   **$200.00**   **8**

Fork Lift Truck, 1960s, M-T Co., 10¼" high, minor toy

    $80.00 $160.00   4

Foto Finish, Racehorse (?), 1950s, M-T Co., 12" long, minor toy

    $120.00 $240.00   8

Four Prop Airplane, 1960s, Waco Co., 17" long, 16¼" wingspan, four actions

    $140.00 $280.00   5

Frankenstein, tin, 1950s, Marx Co., Japan, 12" tall, five actions, remote control
$600.00 $1,200.00+   8

Frankenstein Monster, 1960s, T-N Co., 14" tall, six actions
$140.00 $280.00   2

Frankenstein, 1970s, Poynter Prod., Co., 12" tall, five actions, mostly plastic
$60.00   **$120.00**   **2**

Frankie—The Rollerskating Monkey, 1950s, Alps Co., 12" tall, three actions
$100.00 $200.00   2

Fred Flintstone Bedrock Band, 1962, Alps Co., 9½" high, four actions
$400.00   **$800.00**   **4**

Fred Flintstone on Dino, 1961, Marx Co., Japan, eight actions, 22" long
$350.00 $700.00   4

Fred Flintstone Flivver, 1962, Marx Co., 7" long, minor toy
$400.00 $800.00   7

French Cat, 1950s, Alps Co., 10" long, two cycles, five actions
$50.00 $100.00   6

Friendly Jocko—My Favorite Pet, 1950s, Alps Co., 8" high, five actions, includes detachable cymbals, plastic cup
$150.00 $300.00   8

Friendly Puppy—Barking And Begging, 1950s, Alps Co., 8" long, four actions
$30.00 $60.00   4

Frontier Express, locomotive, 1960s, M-T Co., 15½" long, four actions
$40.00 $80.00   3

Frontier Whistling Locomotive, 1960s, M-T Co., 10" long, three actions
$40.00 $80.00   2

Fruit Juice Counter, 1960s, K Co., 8" long, 8" high, three actions, includes plastic barrel, lid, glasses, and tin tray
$120.00 $240.00   6

Fumbling Pussy, 1970s, M-T Co., 10" long, three actions
$40.00 $80.00   4

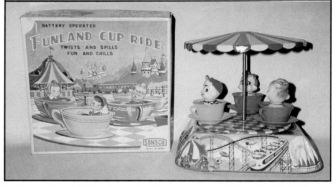

Funland Cup Ride, 1960s, Sonsco Co., 7" tall, 6"x6" base, three actions, includes 6" umbrella
$100.00   **$200.00**   **5**

Funland Loco, 1950s, Daiya Co., 9" long, four actions
$50.00 $100.00   6

Funtime Savings, bank, 1980s, China, 11½" tall, Marilyn Monroe look-alike, minor toy
$30.00 $60.00   2

Galloping Cowboy Savings Bank, 1950s, Y Co., Cragstan, 8" high, 6½" long, minor toy
$450.00 $900.00+   9

Galloping Horse and Rider With 'Hoof Beat' Horse, 1960s, Cragstan Co., 9" long, minor toy
$140.00 $280.00   7

Gama Mercedes Benz 220 SE Sedan, 1960s, Mignon Co., 9" long, three actions

$140.00	$280.00	5

Gear Robot, 1960s, S-H Co., 11½" tall, five actions

$180.00	$360.00	5

Gear Robot, 1960s, Y Co., 10" tall, four actions

$250.00	$500.00	6

General Locomotive, 1950s, Y Co., 9½" long, three actions

$40.00	$80.00	5

General Patton Tank–M-107, 1950s, Daiya Co., 8" long, four actions

$70.00	$140.00	7

Giant Sonic Robot, 1950s, M-T Co., 15" tall, five actions, a.k.a. Train Robot

$2,000.00	$4,000.00+	9

Gino–Neapolitan Balloon Blower, 1960s Tomiyama Co., Rosko, 10" tall, five actions, includes bubble solution plastic tray

$110.00	**$220.00**	**2**

Girl with Baby Carriage, 1960s, T-N Co., 8" high, three actions

$90.00	$180.00	5

Globe Explorer–Savings Bank, 1950s, Wonderful Toy Co., 9" high, 5½" diameter, includes detachable magnetic rocket ship, minor toy

$200.00	$400.00	8

G-Man Machine Gun, 1950s, Exelo Co., 10" long, minor toy

$70.00	$140.00	5

Godzilla, 1960s, Bullmark Co., 10½" tall, five actions

$300.00	$600.00	6

Godzilla Monster, 1970s, Marusan Co., 11½" tall, three actions

$200.00	$400.00	6

Gofer–Robotron, the Mechanical Maniac, 1970, Topper Corp., Japan, 6½" tall, three actions, includes plastic glass and tray, also a bank

$90.00	$180.00	4

Go-Go Girl, bar toy, 1969 Poynter Prod. Co., 15¼" tall, risque toy, PG rated, minor toy

$60.00	$120.00	2

Go Kart, 1960s, M-T Co., 6½" long, includes control wire with steering key, minor toy

$90.00	$180.00	3

Go Kart, 1950s, Rosko Co., 10" long, three actions, includes detachable head

$90.00	$180.00	3

Gold Robot, see Robot, with flashing lighted eyes and moving arms

Golden Gear Robot, 1960s, S-H Co., 9" tall, five actions

$300.00	$600.00	7

Golden Locomotive, 1950s, Nihonkogei Co., 10½" long, minor toy

$40.00	$80.00	3

Gomora Monster, 1960s, Bullmark Co., 8" tall, four actions, includes plastic missiles

$150.00	$300.00	6

Good Time Charlie, 1960s, M-T Co., 12" tall, seven actions

$100.00	**$200.00**	**2**

Gorilla, 1950s, T-N Co., 9¼" tall, five actions, white or brown

$200.00	$400.00	4

Go-Stop Benz Racer, 1950s, Marusan Co., 11" long, three actions

$150.00 $300.00   5

Grace Ocean Liner, 1950s, M-T Co., 15" long, three actions

$250.00 $500.00   5

Grading Tractor, 1950s, Cragstan Co., 7½" long, three actions, minor toy

$60.00 $120.00   6

Grandpa Bear Smoking and Rocking with Pipe Lighted, 1950s, Alps Co., 9" tall, five actions

$150.00 $300.00   4

Grand-Pa Car, 1950s, Y Co., 9" long, four actions

$50.00   **$100.00**   **1**

Grandpa Panda Bear, 1950s, M-T Co., 9" tall, five actions

$140.00 $280.00   4

Great Garloo, The, 1960s, Marx Co., 23" tall, seven actions, includes chain and medallion, mostly plastic

$300.00   **$600.00**   **4**

Green Caterpillar, 1950s, Daiya Co., 19½" long, three actions

$150.00 $300.00   5

Greyhound Bus, 1950s, KKK Co., 7¼" long, minor toy

$90.00   **$180.00**   **4**

Greyhound Bus—Sceni-cruiser, 1950s, I.Y. Metal Toy Co., 16" long, three actions

$90.00 $180.00   3

Greyhound Bus with Headlights, 1950s, Linemar Co., 10¼" long, three actions

$100.00 $200.00   3

Growling Lion Trophy Plaque, 1950s, Cragstan Co., 10" high, three actions

$120.00 $240.00   8

Growling Tiger Trophy Plaque, 1950s, Cragstan Co., 10" high, three actions

$120.00 $240.00   8

Grumman F9F Navy Jet, Cougar, 1950s, K Co., 11½" long, 10¼" wingspan, three actions

$150.00 $300.00   6

Guided Missile Launcher, 1950s, Irco Co., 8" long, 3" tall, 5" wide, three actions, includes plastic missiles

$110.00 $220.00   5

Guided Missile Launcher, 1950s, Y Co., 8¼" long, three actions, includes six plastic missiles

$60.00 $120.00   7

Guided Missile Target Game, 1950s, Alps Co., 14" long, three actions, includes cardboard insert and ammo

$100.00 $200.00   8

Gun With 5 Soldier Tops, 1950s, Linemar Co., 5½" long, minor toy, includes five wooden tops

$90.00 $180.00   9

Gypsy Fortune Teller, 1950s, Ichida Co., 12" high with hat, 5¾" x 7" base, includes 20 fortune cards, five actions

$800.00 $1,600.00+   9

H-O Gauge Electric Train with Real Smoke, 1960s, Amico Co., 23" total length, 17 piece set

$70.00 $140.00   4

Hamburger Chef, 1960s, K Co., 8" long, 8" high, three actions, includes tin frying pan, hamburger, plastic bottles

$110.00 $220.00   3

Hand Car, 1960s, M-T Co., 9¾" long, three actions

$70.00 $140.00   6

Handy-Hank Mystery Tractor, 1950s, T-N Co., 10½" long, four actions

$100.00 $200.00   6

Happy Band Trio, 1970s, M-T Co., 12" high, seven actions

$500.00 $1,000.00   9

Happy Clown Car, 1960s, Y Co., 6½" long, three actions

$100.00 $200.00   5

Happy Clown Theater, with Pinocchio-like puppet, 1950s, Y Co., 10" tall, three actions

$190.00 $380.00   3

Happy Fiddler Clown, The, 1950s, Alps Co., 9½" high, four actions, includes tin litho violin

$230.00 $460.00   4

Happy Miner, 1960s, Bandai Co., 11 tall, three actions

$110.00 $220.00   7

Happy Naughty Chimp, 1960s, Daishin Co., 9½" high assembled, four actions

$50.00 $100.00   5

Happy 'N Sad Magic Face Clown, 1960s, Y Co., 10" tall, five actions

$150.00 $300.00   3

Happy 'N Sad Magic Face Cymbal Clown, 1960s, Y Co., 10" tall, five actions

$200.00 $400.00   5

Happy Plane, 1960s, TPS Co., 9" long, 10½" wingspan, three actions

$75.00 $150.00   2

Happy Santa, 1960s, Z Co., 11" tall, three actions

$100.00 $200.00   2

Happy Santa, stands and sits on a chimney, 1960s, Zawa Co., 12½" tall standing, 10" sitting, four actions

$200.00 $400.00   7

Happy Santa, Walking, 1950s, Alps Co., 11" tall, five actions
$150.00 $300.00   **3**

Happy Santa With Lighted Eyes, 1950s, Alps Co., 9" high, six actions, includes cymbals, stand, and drum
$140.00 $280.00   3

Happy Singing Bird, 1950s, M-T Co., 9" high, bird 3" long, 5⅝" dia. base, three actions
$60.00 $120.00   3

Happy the Clown Puppet Show, with Pinocchio-like puppet, 1960s, Y Co., 10" tall, three actions
$190.00 $380.00   **3**

Happy Tractor, 1960s, Daiya Co., 8" long, four actions
$40.00 $80.00   3

Harbor Patrol B-390, gunboat, 1950s, Bandai Co., 9" long, four actions
$70.00 $140.00   6

Harbor Patrol Boat, 1950s, I.T.O . Co., 22" long, minor toy
$300.00 $600.00   8

Harbor-Queen Boat, 1950s, M-T Co., 12" long, minor toy
$150.00 $300.00   4

Hasty Chimp, 1970s, Y Co., 12" tall, four actions, mostly plastic
$30.00$60.00   3

Haunted House Mystery Bank, 1960s, Disneyland promotions, Brumberger Co., 7⅝" high, four actions
$250.00 $500.00   3

Heavy-Duty Bulldozer, 1950s, T-N Co., 11" long, five actions
$150.00 $300.00   6

Heavy Machine Gun, 1950s, T-N Co., 24" long, 13" high on tripod, four actions, includes detachable tripod and plastic ammo belt
$100.00 $200.00   4

Her—The Sad Eyed Dog, 1960s, Frankonia Co., 11" long nose to tail tip, five actions, two cycles
$50.00 $100.00   7

Hi Bouncer Moon Scout, robot, 1968, Marx Co., 11¼" tall, five actions, includes five plastic balls
$450.00 $900.00   7

High Jinks of the Circus, 1950s, T-N Co., 14" high, extends to 29", six actions
$200.00 $400.00   2

Highway Drive, 1950s, T-N Co., 15½" long, three actions, includes tin magnetic cat
$70.00 $140.00   2

Highway Patrol, 1950s, M-T Co., 11¾" long, seven actions
$400.00 $800.00   **5**

Highway Patrol Copter, 1960s, M-T Co., 9½" long, four actions, includes detachable plastic rotor

    $100.00 $200.00   5

Highway Patrol Police Special, 1960s, Y Co., five actions, 11½" long

    $100.00   **$200.00**   **2**

Highway Patrol Jeep, 1950s, Daiya Co., 10" long, four actions

    $70.00 $140.00   2

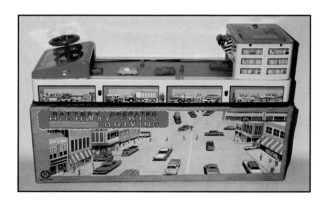

Highway Skill Driving, 1960s, K Co., 13" long, three actions

    $70.00   **$140.00**   **2**

Hiller Hornet Helicopter, 1950s, Alps Co., 12¼" long, 15", two piece metal rotor, four actions

    $120.00 $240.00   3

Him—The Sad Eyed Dog, 1960s, Frankonia Co., 11" long, nose to tail tip, five actions, two cycles

    $50.00 $100.00   7

Hi-Power Speed Boat, with outboard motor, G—W Co., 12" long, minor toy

    $80.00 $160.00   8

Hippo Chef, Cuty Cook, 1960s, Y Co., 10" tall, five actions, includes chef hat and tin litho egg

    $150.00 $300.00+   8

Hole-In-One Bank, 1960s, no marking, 8½" long x 3½" wide, minor toy, includes marked test coin and golfer

    $70.00   **$140.00**   **2**

Holiday Sink—Stove Combination, 1950s, T-N Co., 9" high, minor toy, includes three piece pan set

    $40.00 $80.00   3

Home Washing Machine, 1950s, Y Co., 6" high, minor toy

    $40.00 $80.00   6

Honeymoon Car With Music, 1960s, T-N Co., 10½" long, three actions, plays "Here Comes The Bride"

    $270.00   **$540.00**   **9**

Hoop Zing Girl, 1950s, Linemar Co., 11½" tall, minor toy

    $150.00 $300.00   5

Hoopy the Fishing Duck, 1950s, Alps Co., 10" high, seven actions, includes magnetic fish and detachable pond

    $250.00 $500.00   7

Hootin' Hollow Haunted House, 1960s, Marx, 11" high, eight actions

    $500.00 $1,000.00+   5

Hooting Locomotive, 1950s, M-T Co., 9" long, minor toy

    $30.00 $60.00   3

Hooty the Happy Owl, 1960s, Alps Co., 9" tall, six actions
$90.00 $180.00   3

Hopping Pup With Cart, 1950s, Alps Co., 14" long, 9" high, three actions
$40.00 $80.00   7

Hop Up Boat, 1960s, M-T Co., 9" long, three actions, includes detachable captain figure
$40.00 $80.00   7

Hot Rod, (Dream Boat), 1950s, T-N Co., 7" long, three actions
$160.00 $320.00   3

Hot Rod Custom 'T' Ford, 1960s, Alps Co., 10½" long, four actions
$180.00 $360.00   3

Hot Rod—15B, 1950s, T-N Co., 10" long, four actions
$200.00 $400.00   9

Hot Rod Limousine, 1960s, Alps Co., 10½" long, four actions
$180.00 $360.00   4

Hot Rod Racer #7, 1950s, K Co., 9" long, five actions
$80.00 $160.00   8

Hot Rod 777—Lumar Special, 1950s, Marx Co., 11" long, three actions, friction with lights
$90.00 $180.00   8

Hungry Baby Bear, 1950s, Y Co., 9½" tall, six actions
$180.00 $360.00   2

Hungry Cat, 1960s, Linemar Co., 9" high, seven actions, includes tin tray and plastic fish
$350.00 $700.00   8

Hungry Hound Dog, 1950s, Y Co., 9½" high, six actions
$190.00 $380.00   7

Hungry Sheep, 1950s, M-T Co., 9" long, three actions, two cycles
$100.00 $200.00   6

Hy-Que Monkey, 1960s, T-N Co., 17" tall, six actions
$150.00 $300.00   2

Ice Cream Baby Bear, 1950s, M-T Co., 9½" high, three actions, chocolate
$200.00 $400.00   8

Ice Cream Baby Bear, 1950s, M-T Co., 9½" high, three actions, vanilla
$220.00 $440.00   9

Ice Cream Vendor, 1950s, T-N Co., 9" long, five actions
$250.00 $500.00   7

Indian Joe, 1960s, Alps Co., 12" tall, four actions
$80.00 $160.00   2

Indian Signal Choo Choo, 1960s, Kanto Toys Co., 9½" long, four actions
$80.00 $160.00   5

Interceptor, target game, 1950s, S&E Co., 13" high, 16" wingspan, four actions
$150.00 $300.00   7

Interplanet Space Fleet Gun, see Space Pilot Super-Sonic Gun

Interplanetary Rocket, 1960s, Y Co., 14¾" tall, five actions
    $120.00 $240.00   5

Interplanetary Space Fighter, 1960s, T-N Co., 12" long, four actions, V-7 Super Jet
    $400.00 $800.00   7

Iron Horse, 1950s, M-T Co., 14" long, five actions
    $50.00 $100.00   7

JDN 7673 Sedan—4 door, 1920s, Distler Co., one of the earliest battery operated toys, 14" long, minor toy
    $400.00 $800.00   10

Jack 'N' Jill Action Rail Car, 1960s, Hong Kong, 9" high, three actions, 15 piece set, mostly plastic
    $60.00 $120.00   8

Jack-O-Lantern, lantern toy, 1950s, Amico Co., 3½" tall, minor toy
    $30.00   **$60.00**   **1**

Jaguar X-77, tank, 1950s, Daiya Co., 9½" long, three actions, includes ammunition
    $70.00 $140.00   6

Jalopy, 1950s, Linemar Co., 7½" long, three actions
    $100.00 $200.00   5

James Bond's Aston-Martin, 1966, Gilbert Co., 11½" long, eight actions, includes ejectable passenger
    $250.00 $500.00   3

Jeep—USA, 1950s, TKK Co., 12½" long, minor toy
    $70.00 $140.00   4

Jeep No. 10560, 1950s, Cragstan, 5½" long, a minor action toy
    $70.00 $140.00   4

Jeepster, 1960s, Daiya Co., 10" long, minor toy
    $60.00 $120.00   4

Jet Airport with 4 Jet Airplanes, 1960s, Turnpike Lines, Sears, 12½" long, seven actions
    $150.00 $300.00   7

Jet Plane with Smoking and Tail Light, 1950s, T-N Co., 13" long, 12" wingspan, four actions, 40 piece set with 39 punchout figures
    $150.00 $300.00   8

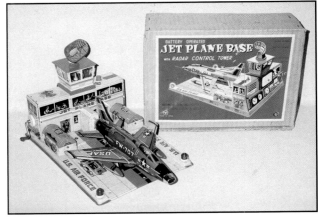

Jet Plane Base, 1950s, Y Co., 7¼" x 11" base, plane 9" long, 7" wingspan, seven actions, includes crank
    $450.00   **$900.00**   **8**

Jetrail Express, monorail, 1960s, Northrop Products—U.S.A., 12" long, minor toy, includes 12 support towers and wire track
    $60.00 $120.00   8

Jetspeed Racer, 1960s, Y Co., 17½" long, three actions
    $150.00 $300.00   8

Jig-Saw-Magic, 1950s, Z Co., 7¼" high, 4½" x 8½", minor action toy
    $40.00 $80.00   3

Jocko the Drinking Monkey, 1950s, Linemar, 11" tall, four actions, includes top hat
    $90.00 $180.00   1

Johnny Speedmobile, 1960s, Remco Co., 15" long, 8¾" high, three actions, mostly plastic
    $140.00 $280.00   8

John's Farm Truck, 1950s, T-N Co., 9" long, seven actions
    $100.00 $200.00   2

Jo-Jo the Flipping Monkey, 1970s, T-N Co., Illfelder, 10" high, minor toy
    $50.00 $100.00   2

Jolly Bambino, 1950s, Alps Co., 9" high, five actions, includes candy pieces
    $300.00 $600.00   5

Jolly Bear the Drummer Boy, 1950s, K Co., 7" tall, five actions
$150.00 $300.00   6

Jolly Bear with Robin, 1950s, M-T Co., 10" tall, three actions
$300.00 $600.00+   10

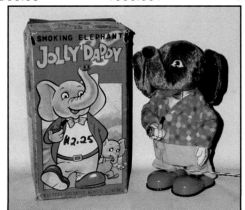

Jolly Daddy Smoking Elephant, 1950s, Marusan Co., 8¾" tall, four actions
$160.00 $320.00   6

Jolly Drummer Chimpy, 1950s, Alps Co., 9" high, six actions, includes cymbals and stand
$80.00 $160.00   4

Jolly Drumming Bear, 1950s, T-N Co., 7" tall, four actions
$70.00 $140.00   5

Jolly Popcorn Vendor, 1960s, T-N Co., 8" long, 9" high, four actions
$160.00 $320.00   7

Jolly Penguin, 1950s, T-N Co., 7" tall, five actions
$100.00 $200.00   6

Jolly Pianist, see Beethoven—The Piano Playing Dog

Jolly Santa on Snow, 1950s, Alps Co., 12½" tall, four actions, two cycles, includes tin skis
$150.00 $300.00   5

Josie the Walking Cow, 1950s, Daiya Co., 14" long, 8½" high, seven actions, two cycles
$120.00 $240.00   2

Journey Pup, c.1950s, S&E Co., 7½" long, four actions, remote control
$50.00 $100.00   3

Jumbo the Bubble Blowing Elephant, 1950s, Y Co., 7½" high, three actions, includes plastic bowl for bubble solution
$80.00 $160.00   1

Jungle Jumbo, 1950s, B–C Toy Co., 10" long, six actions, two cycles, includes detachable Teddy Roosevelt hunter
$300.00 $600.00   10

Jungle Trio, 1950s, Linemar, 8" high, eight actions, includes detachable tin litho whistle
$500.00 $1,000.00+   8

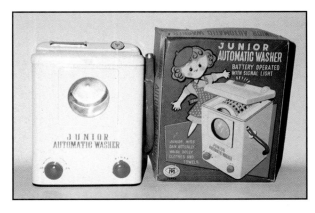

Junior Automatic Washer, 1950s, M-T Co., 6½" high, minor toy
$30.00 $60.00   5

Jupiter Jyro Set, 1970s, Tomy Co., 13" high assembled, minor toy, eight piece set, spaceship 5" diameter, mostly plastic
$80.00 $160.00   8

Jupiter Robot, 1950s, Yonezawa Co., 12¾" tall, four actions
$1,000.00 $2,000.00+   8

Jupiter Rocket Launching Pad, 1960s, T-N Co., 8½" long, 7" high, four actions

      $190.00 $380.00   6

K-55 Electric Tractor, c.1950s, M-T Co., 7" long, three actions

      $70.00 $140.00   4

Kiddie Trolley, 1960s, M-T Co., 7¾" long, five actions

      $50.00 $100.00   5

King Flying Saucer, 1960s, K.O. Co., 7½" diameter, three actions

      $70.00 $140.00   4

King Size Fire Engine, 1960s, Bandai Co., 12½" long, three actions

      $150.00 $300.00   4

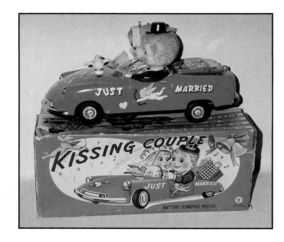

Kissing Couple, 1950s, Ichida Co., 10¾" long, five actions

      $150.00   **$300.00**   **3**

Kitchen-ette Stove and Sink, 1940s, no marking, 6½" long x 6¾" high, minor toy, includes kitchen utensils and side tray and stoppers

      $50.00 $100.00   4

Knight in Armor Target Game, 1950s, M-T Co., 12" tall, three actions, includes crossbow and rubber tipped darts

      $200.00 $400.00   8

Knitting Grandma, 1950s, T-N Co., 8½" tall, three actions

      $140.00 $280.00   5

Kooky–Spooky Whistling Tree, see Whistling Spooky Kooky Tree

Krome Dome, robot, see Martin the Martian

Ladder Fire Engine, 1950s, Linemar Co., 13" long, five actions

      $170.00 $340.00   6

Ladder Fire Engine, 1960s, Asahi Toy Co., 8" long, four actions

      $90.00 $180.00   4

Ladder Fire Truck, 1950s, T-N Co., 12¼" long, five actions

      $150.00 $300.00   5

Lady Pup Tending Her Garden, 1950s, Cragstan Co., 8" high, five actions

      $170.00   **$340.00**   **5**

Lambo, with Magnetic Trunk and Light, 1950s, Alps Co., 16" long with trailer, seven actions, includes two tin logs and trailer

      $250.00 $500.00   9

Laughing Robot, 1970s, Y Co., 9½" tall, three actions, mostly plastic

      $60.00   **$120.00**   **2**

Lavender Robot, see Non-Stop Robot

'Lectric Revolver, 1950s, Daisy Mfg. Co., 11½" long, three actions

      $40.00 $80.00   4

Leo—the Growling Pet Lion with Magic Face-Change, 1970s, Tomiyama Co., 9" long, 2 cycles, three actions
$100.00 $200.00   **5**

Lift Truck, 1950s, M-T Co., 11½" long, 8" high, three actions, includes detachable tin driver
$120.00 $240.00   6

Light House, 1950s, Alps Co., 8½" high, 6¾" x 6¾" base, five actions, includes detachable spinball tower
$800.00 $1,600.00+   10

Light—Prop Flying Tiger, 1960s, M-T Co., 9" long, 9" wingspan, three actions
$100.00 $200.00   8

Lighted Freight Train, 1950s, Y Co., four actions, 25½" long, five pieces, 8 section track
$70.00 $140.00   5

Lighted Space Vehicle with Floating Satellite, 1960s, M-T Co., 8½" long, three actions, includes cell ball
$150.00 $300.00   5

Linda Lee Laundromat, washing machine, 1940s, T-N Co., 6½" high, minor toy
$40.00 $80.00   3

Linemar Music Hall, 1950s, Linemar Co., 8" high, 7¾" x 5½" base, four actions
$150.00 $300.00   5

Lion, 1950s, Linemar, 9" long, four actions
$70.00 $140.00   5

Lion Target Game, 1950s, M-T Co., 7½" high, four actions, includes dart gun and darts
$120.00 $240.00   6

Lite-It-Up-Ford, 1950s, Ichiko Co., 7½" long, minor toy
$110.00 $220.00   8

Lite-O-Wheel Go Kart, 1950s, Rosko Dist. Co., 10" long, three actions, includes detachable vinyl boy's head
$100.00 $200.00   2

Lite-O-Wheel Lincoln, 1950s, Rosko Dist. Co., 10½" long, minor toy
$150.00 $300.00   5

Lite-Up-Telephone Bear, 1950s, M-T Co., 8" high, four actions
$150.00 $300.00   8

Lited Piston Action Plane, 1950s, T-N Co., 14" long, 12" wingspan, three actions
$150.00 $300.00   5

Little Indian, 1960s, T-N Co., 9" tall, three actions
$80.00 $160.00   8

Locomotive—Continental Blue, 1970s, M-T Co., 13" long, four actions
$40.00 $80.00   1

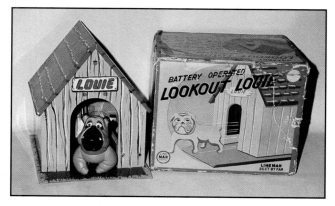

Lookout Louie, 1950s, Linemar Co., 6½" high, minor toy, includes vinyl dog
$60.00 $120.00   4

Loop Plane, (Swallow), 1950s, M-T Co., 9" long, 9" wingspan, four actions
$100.00 $200.00   7

Loop-the-Loop Clown, 1960s, T–N Co., 10" high, minor toy

| $60.00 | $120.00 | 5 |

Loop-the-Loop Monkey, 1960s, T–N Co., 10" high, minor toy

| $50.00 | $100.00 | 5 |

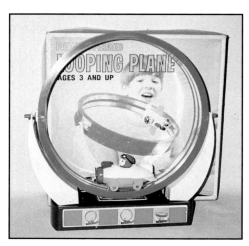

Looping Plane, c.1960s, Y Co., Sears distributor, 14½" high, airplane 5" long, 5 piece set, mostly plastic, minor toy

| $60.00 | $120.00 | 6 |

Looping Space Tank, 1960s, Daiya Co., 8" long, five actions

| $100.00 | $200.00 | 7 |

Los Walky-Son, 1960s, Geyper Co., 11½" high, 15" wide, includes detachable rifles and baton

| $120.00 | $240.00 | 7 |

Lost in Space Robot, 1966, Remco Co., 13" tall, three actions, mostly plastic

| $200.00 | $400.00 | 2 |

Love-Beetle-Volks, 1960s, K.O. Co., 10" long, three actions

| $60.00 | $120.00 | 2 |

Lucky Crane, 1950s, M-T Co., 8½" high, five actions, includes tin prizes

| $500.00 | $1,000.00 | 9 |

Lucky Locomotive, 1950s, Marusan Co., 8" long, four actions

| $40.00 | $80.00 | 2 |

Lucky Mixer, cement truck, 1960s, M-T Co., 12" long, four actions

| $70.00 | $140.00 | 6 |

Lucky Seven—Dice Throwing Monkey, 1960s, Alps Co., 11½" tall, five actions, includes plastic straw hat, five dice, two game sheets, twenty chips

| $100.00 | $200.00 | 3 |

Lufthansa Jet Airplane, 1960s, GAMA Co., 19½" long, 18½" wingspan, three actions

| $110.00 | $220.00 | 7 |

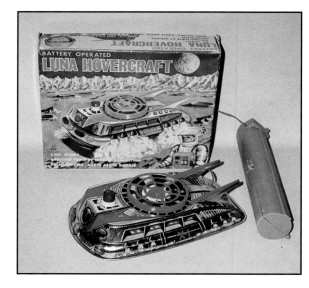

Luna Hovercraft, 1960s, TPS Co., 7" long, three actions

| $60.00 | $120.00 | 7 |

Lunar Captain, 1960s, T–N Co., 13½" long extended, five actions

$110.00	$220.00	6

Lunar Loop/Swing and Orbiting Action, 1960s, Daiya Co., 14" high, 12" diameter hoop, three actions

$100.00	$200.00	6

Lunar Patrol, 1960s, Cragston Co., 11" long, five actions, a.k.a. Cragstan Space Mobile, includes detachable plastic antenna

$250.00	$500.00	8

Lunar Spaceman, 1960s, Mego Co., 12" tall, five actions

$100.00	$200.00	5

Luncheonette Bank, 1960s, K Co., 8" long, 8" high, three actions, includes plastic condiments

$160.00	$320.00	8

M-101 Aston Martin Secret Ejector Car, 1960s, Daiya Co., 11" long, six actions, includes ejectable passenger

$200.00	**$400.00**	**7**

Mac the Turtle with the Barrel, 1960s, Y Co., 8" high, five actions

$100.00	**$200.00**	**3**

Machine Man Robot, 1950s, M-T Co., 15" tall, four actions

$4,000.00	$8,000.00+	10

Machine Robot, 1960s, S–H Co., 12" high, six actions

$250.00	$500.00	6

Magic Action Bulldozer, 1950s, T–N Co., 9½" long, three actions

$100.00	$200.00	3

Magic Man, Clown, 1950s, Marusan Co., 11" tall, five actions

$260.00	**520.00**	**4**

Magic Snowman, 1950s, M-T Co., Santa Creations, 11¼" tall, four actions, includes detachable tin broom, plastic pipe and styro ball

$150.00	$300.00	3

Magnet Rail Orbiter, 1960s, Y Co., 14" high, 12" diameter, minor toy

$70.00	$140.00	4

Mainstreet, 1950s, Linemar Co., 19½" long, three actions
   $500.00   **$1,000.00+**   **10**

Major Tooty, 1960s, Alps Co., R. F., 14" tall, three actions, includes drum and hat
   $100.00 $200.00   4

Make-Up Bear, 1960s, M-T Co., 9" high, four actions
   $500.00   **$1,000.00**   **9**

Mambo—The Jolly Drumming Elephant, 1950s, Alps Co., 9½" high, six actions, includes drum, cymbals, and stand
   $150.00   **$300.00**   **4**

Man In Space, 1960s, Alps Co., 8" long battery box with 7" long Space Man, minor toy
   $400.00 $800.00   9

Man-Made Satellite, 19650s, SKK Co., Hofu, 8⅜" long, five actions, includes detachable tin moon and tin satellite
   $200.00 $400.00   8

Marching Bear, 1960s, Alps Co., 10" tall, five actions
   $60.00 $120.00   2

Mars Explorer, Astronaut, 1960s, S–H Co., 10" tall, six actions
   $250.00 $500.00   6

Mars Explorer, Robot, 1950s, S–H Co., 9½" tall, seven actions
   $200.00 $400.00   5

Mars King, Astronaut, 1960s, S–H Co., 9½" tall, four actions
   $400.00 $800.00   7

Mars King–Robot No. 12101, 1960s, S–H Co., 9½" tall, four actions
   $450.00 $900.00   8

Mars Spaceship, (?), 1950s, M-T Co., 14½" long, three actions
   $170.00 $340.00   8

Marshal Wild Bill, 1950s, Y Co., 10½" tall, four actions, two cycles, includes tin cowboy hat
   $180.00   **$360.00**   **2**

Martian Robot, 1970s, SJM Co., 12" tall, four actions
   $60.00 $120.00   2

Martin the Martian, a.k.a. Krome Dome Robot, 1960s, Yonezawa Co., 10½" tall, four actions

    $350.00 $700.00   8

Marvelous Car, T-Bird, 1956, T–N Co., 11" long, three actions

    $250.00 $500.00   4

Marvelous Fire Engine, 1960s, Y Co., 11" long, four actions

    $100.00   **$200.00**   **3**

Marvelous Locomotive, 1950s, T–N Co., 10" long, four actions, includes detachable smokestack and two styro balls

    $80.00   **$160.00**   **8**

Marvelous Mike, 1950s, Saunders Co., 17" long, four actions

    $150.00 $300.00   3

Mary's Little Lamb, 1950s, Alps Co., 10½" high, three actions

    $100.00 $200.00   8

Maxwell Coffee-Loving Bear, 1960s, T–N Co., 10" tall, five actions

    $120.00 $240.00   2

McGregor, 1960s, T–N Co., 12" tall when standing, six actions

    $100.00   **$200.00**   **1**

Mechanic Robot, 1960s, S–T Co., 12" tall, five actions

    $150.00 $300.00   5

Mechanized Robot, The, 1950s, T–N Co., 13½" tall, four actions, a.k.a. Robbie

    $400.00   **$800.00**   **2**

Melody Camping Car, 1970s, Y Co., 10" long, three actions

    $60.00 $120.00   3

Melody Train, 1966, Matsuzo Kosuge Co., Frankonia, 6½" long, minor toy, includes six sections of track and 48 xylophone bars

    $40.00 $80.00   4

Mercury Cougar ('68 Mercury), 1968, Taiyo Co., 10" long, minor toy

$60.00	$120.00	4

Mercury Explorer—Magic Color Dome, 1960s, TPS Co., 8" long, five actions

$120.00	**$240.00**	**3**

Mercury X-1—Space Saucer, 1960s, Y Co., includes detachable antenna, 8" diameter, four actions

$70.00	$140.00	2

Merry Christmas, Santa In His Rockin' Chair, 1950s, Alps Co., three actions, 21" tall assembled, includes detachable tree and stocking

$500.00	$1,000.00+	9

Merry-Go-Round Truck, 1950s, T–N Co., 11" long, four actions

$250.00	**$500.00**	**6**

Merry-Go-Round Truck #700, 1957, T–N Co., 8½" long, four actions, remote control

$250.00	$500.00	7

Merry Rabbit, 1950s, K Co., 11" tall, five actions

$100.00	$200.00	9

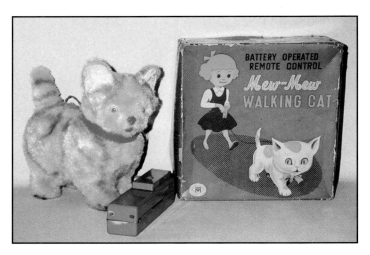

Mew-Mew Walking Cat, 1950s, M-T Co., 7" long, six actions

$60.00	**$120.00**	**9**

Mexicali Pete—The Drum Player, 1960s, Alps Co., 10½" high, three actions

$60.00	$120.00	3

Mickey Mouse and Donald Duck Fire Engine, 1960s, M-T Co., 16" long, four actions

$500.00	$1,000.00+	8

Mickey Mouse Locomotive, 1960s, M-T Co., 9" long, six actions

$150.00	**$300.00**	**5**

Mickey Mouse Melody Railroad, 1960s, Frankonia Co., minor toy, 6¾" long, handcar, includes four circular rails with xylophone bars

$500.00	$1,000.00+	9

Mickey Mouse on Handcar, 1960s, M-T Co., 9¾" long, 7¾" high, three actions

$160.00	$320.00	4

Mickey Mouse Sand Buggy, 1960s, M-T Co., 11" long, four actions

$150.00 $300.00   4

Mickey Mouse Scooter, 1960s, M-T Co., 8" long, three actions

$160.00 $320.00   4

Mickey Mouse Talking Telephone, 1964, Hasbro Co., 12" high, minor toy, includes two records

$90.00 $180.00   7

Mickey Mouse Tow Truck, 1960s, Andy Gard Co., 7½" long, minor toy

$300.00   **$600.00**   **6**

Mickey Mouse Trolley, 1960s, M-T Co., 11" high, three actions

$150.00 $300.00   6

Mickey the Magician, 1960s, Linemar, 10" tall, four actions, includes tin chick

$1,000.00 $2,000.00+   7

Mighty 8 Robot with Magic Color, 1960s, M-T Co., 12" tall, four actions

$1,200.00 $2,400.00+   10

Mighty Kong, 1950s, Marx, 11" tall, five actions

$300.00   **$600.00**   **3**

Mighty Kong Big Mouth—Ball Blowing Game, 1950s, Marx Co., 13" high assembled, minor toy, includes tin dart gun, two darts, two styrofoam balls

$300.00 $600.00   9

Mighty Mike the Barbell Lifter Bear, 1950s, K Co., 10½" tall, four actions

$150.00   **$300.00**   **4**

Mighty Robot, 1960s, K-O Co., 11½" tall, four actions

$900.00 $1,800.00   9

Military Air Defense Truck, 1950s, Linemar Co., 15¼" long, four actions

$100.00 $200.00   5

Military Command Car, 1950s, T–N Co., 11" long, five actions

$150.00 $300.00   5

Military Jet Plane, 1960s, Marx Co., 14" long, 14½" wingspan, three actions

$100.00   **$200.00**   **4**

Military Police Car, 1950s, Linemar, 7" long, four actions

$100.00 $200.00   4

Million Bus, 1950s, KKK Co., 12" long, three actions
$1,250.00 $2,500.00+   9

Mimi Poodle with Bone, 1950s, T–N Co., 11" long, 10" high, five actions, two cycles, includes plastic bone
$50.00 $100.00   3

Mischievous Monkey, 1950s, M-T Co., 13" tall, six actions, includes tree and monkey
$300.00   **$600.00**   **5**

Miss Friday—The Typist, 1950s, T–N Co., 8" tall, six actions, removable vinyl head
$150.00   **$300.00**   **2**

Missile Robot, 1970s, S–H Co., 9" tall, four actions, includes four plastic darts or rockets
$60.00 $120.00   3

Missile Robot—Mr. 45, M-T Co., 17½" tall, five actions
$100.00 $200.00   4

Mr. Atom—The Electronic Walking Robot, 1950s, Advance Doll & Toy Co., 17" tall, six actions
$200.00 $400.00   6

Mr. Atomic Robot, 1950s, Cragstan, 11" tall, three actions, original
$2,500.00 $5,000.00+   9

Mr. Baseball Junior, 1950s, K Co., 7" high, three actions, with game box and eight plastic balls
$450.00   **$900.00**   **7**

Mr. Chief, Robot, 1950s, K-O Co., 12" tall, four actions
$450.00 $900.00   8

Mr. Fox The Magician Blowing Magical Bubbles, 1960s, Y Co., 9" tall, five actions, includes plastic dish
$200.00   **$400.00**   **6**

Mr. Fox the Magician—with the Magical Disappearing Rabbit, 1960s, Y Co., 9" tall, five actions, includes plastic rabbit
$300.00 $600.00   7

Mr. Hustler Robot, 1960s, Taiyo Co., 11" tall, six actions

$200.00 $400.00 6

Mr. MacPooch, Taking a Walk and Smoking His Pipe, 1950s, SAN Co., 8" tall, four actions

$130.00 $260.00 4

Mr. Magoo Car, 1961, Hubley Co., 9" long, five actions, includes cloth roof top

$200.00 **$400.00** **2**

Mr. Mars, Astronaut, 1960s, S–H Co., 11½" tall, five actions, two cycles

$200.00 $400.00 7

Mr. Mercury, Type I, all tin, 1960s, Marx Co., 13" tall, seven actions

$300.00 **$600.00** **3**

Mr. Mercury, Type II, lighted, 1960s, Marx Co., 13" tall, 7 actions

$250.00 $500.00 3

Mr. Patrol—with Siren, 1960s, S–H Co., 12" tall, five actions, astronaut

$160.00 $320.00 7

Mister Robot, 1970s, Cragstan Co., 11" tall, three actions, mostly plastic, Mr. Robot on chest

$200.00 $400.00 7

Mr. Robot the Mechanical Brain, 1950s, Alps Co., three actions, 8" tall

$600.00 $1,200.00 8

Mr. Strong Pup—Mighty Weightlifter, 1950s, K Co., 9" tall, five actions

$150.00 $300.00 5

Mr. Zerox, 1960s, S–H Co., 9½" tall, four actions

$150.00 $300.00 5

Mix-ette Mixer, 1940s, KDP Co., 9" high when assembled, minor toy, includes mixer stand and bowl

$30.00 $60.00 3

Mobile Artillery Unit, 1950s, T–N Co., 10" long, four actions

$150.00 $300.00 6

Mobile Satellite Tracking Station, 1960s, Y Co., six actions, 9" long, includes detachable antenna

$400.00 $800.00 6

Mobile Space T.V. Unit with Trailer, 1960s, T–N Co., 10½" long assembled, six actions

$500.00 $1,000.00+ 8

Moby Dick Whaling Boat, 1950s, Linemar Co., 12" long, three actions, remote control

$150.00 $300.00 8

Mod Monster—Blushing Frankenstein, 1960s, T–N Co., 13¼" tall, five actions

$150.00 $300.00 2

Model Motor Boat, 1950s, S–W Co., 11" long, minor toy

$80.00 $160.00 4

Model Motor-Boat, 1950s, I.T.O. Co., 18" long, minor toy, mostly wood, includes stand

$110.00 $220.00 8

Model Motorboat, 1950s, S–W Co., 9½" long, minor toy, mostly wood

$60.00 $120.00 4

Modern Robot, 1950s, Yoshiya Co., 10½" tall, four actions

$600.00 $1,200.00 8

Mond Robot #2001, Lunar Spaceman, Hong Kong, 12" tall, five actions

  $150.00   **$300.00**   **7**

Monkee Mobile, 1967, ASC Co., (Aoshin Co.), 12" long, minor toy

  $300.00   **$600.00**   **5**

Monkey Handcar, 1950s, T–N Co., 7" high, three actions

  $150.00 $300.00   6

Monkey On A Picnic, 1950s, Alps Co., 9½" high, seven actions

  $200.00 $400.00   7

Monkey The Shoe Maker, 1950s, T–N Co., 9" high, three actions

  $300.00 $600.00   8

Monorail Rocket Ship, 1950s, Linemar Co., 10" long, with supports and rail rods, minor toy

  $140.00 $280.00   5

Monster Robot, 1970s, S–H Co., 10" tall, three actions

  $70.00 $140.00   4

Monsturn, see Turn Signal Robot

Moon Astronaut, 1950s, Daiya Co., 9" tall, four actions

  $500.00 $1,000.00   9

Moon Car With Light And Mystery Action, 1960s, T–N Co., 12½" long, 8" high, four actions

  $500.00 $1,000.00+   6

Moon Detector, 1960s, Y Co., 10½" long, six actions

  $400.00 $800.00   9

Moon Explorer, 1950s, Ideal Co., 25" long, four actions, includes three plastic darts

  $70.00 $140.00   3

Moon Explorer, M-27, 1960s, Yonezawa Co., 9" long, 7" high, five actions, includes detachable antenna

  $350.00 $700.00   7

Moon Explorer, Robot, 1960s, Bandai Co., 17½" tall feet to antenna top, five actions

  $600.00 $1,200.00   8

Moon Explorer, Vehicle, 1960s, Gakken Co., five actions, 11" long

  $150.00 $300.00   5

Moon Explorer, 1960s, M-T Co., 14" long, three actions

  $250.00 $500.00   7

Moon Express, Magic Color, 1950s, TPS Co., 12" long, four actions

  $120.00   **$240.00**   **3**

Moon Globe Orbiter, c.1960s, Y Co., (Mego) three actions, rocket orbits globe, noise, lights, 10½" high

  $100.00 $200.00   4

Moon Grabber, 1960s, Marx Co., 8" long, minor toy

  $40.00 $80.00   3

Moon Man 001, 1960s, Hong Kong, 6" tall, minor toy, mostly plastic

  $90.00 $180.00   8

Moon Orbiter, 1960s, Y Co., 4" long, includes six sections of track and trestles, minor toy

    $120.00 $240.00   5

Moon Patrol 11, 1960s, Y Co., 8" diameter, four actions

    $60.00 $120.00   5

Moon Patrol–Space Division No. 3, see Moon Car With Light and Mystery Action

Moon Patrol, 1960s, Gakken Toy Co., 11½" long, five actions, includes two antenna and a transmitter

    $140.00   **$280.00**   **5**

Moon Rocket, 1950s, M-T Co., 9" long, three actions, includes detachable plastic astronaut

    $140.00 $280.00   5

Moon Rocket, 1950s, Y Co., 15¼" long, three actions

    $400.00 $800.00   7

Moon Rocket–XM-12, 1960s, Y Co., 14½" long, four actions

    $320.00 $640.00   9

Moon Ship, 1970s, Tomy Toy Co., 8½" diameter, three actions, includes styro spaceman, capsule, and balloons

    $40.00 $80.00   3

Moon Space Ship, 1950s, T–N Co., 13" long, five actions

    $1,000.00 $2,000.00+   10

Moon Traveler–Apollo Z, 1960s, T–N Co., 12" long, 15" extended, five actions

    $120.00 $240.00   4

Mother Bear–Sitting and Knitting In Her Old Rocking Chair, 1950s, M-T. Co., 9½" high, four actions

    $170.00 $340.00   5

Motor Boat, 1950s, Fleet Line Co., 12" long, minor toy, mostly wood

    $80.00 $160.00   4

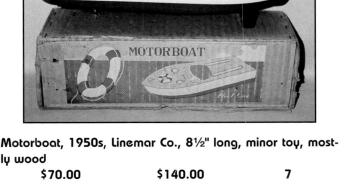

Motorboat, 1950s, Linemar Co., 8½" long, minor toy, mostly wood

    $70.00   **$140.00**   **7**

Motorcycle Cop, 1950s, Daiya Co., 10½" long, 8¼" high, five actions

    $300.00 $600.00   7

Mountain Cable Car, 1950s, Cragstan Co., 9" long, minor toy, includes cable

    $60.00 $120.00   5

Movieland Drive-In Theater, 1959, Remco Co., 14" long, includes six small cars and cards, filmstrips, minor toy

    $75.00 $150.00   2

Multi-Action Lockheed Prop-Jet, 1950s, Y Co., 15¼" long, 14" wingspan, five actions, with sequential spinning propellers

    $130.00 $260.00   4

Multi Actions Electra Jet–KLM Royal Dutch Airlines PH–DSF, 1960s, T–N Co., 14" long, 17" wingspan, three actions

    $110.00 $220.00   5

Mumbo Jumbo, Hawaiian Drummer, 1960s, Alps Co., 9¾" high, three actions

    $100.00   **$200.00**   **5**

Musical Bank–Organ Grinder and Dancing Monkey, 1950s, HTC Co., 8" tall, four actions, includes test coin and detachable celluloid monkey

$500.00 $1,000.00+   10

Musical Bear, 1950s, Linemar Co., 10" tall, six actions, including detachable tin horn, drum, and cymbals

$300.00 $600.00   7

Musical Bulldog Playing Piano, 1950s, SAN Co., 8½" tall, 6" x 9" base, four actions

$600.00 $1,200.00   8

Musical Cadillac Car, 1950s, Irco Co., 9" long, minor toy

$200.00 $400.00   5

Musical Car W/Music Box, 1950s, Asahitoy Co., 8¾" long, minor toy, plays "There's No Place Like Home"

$150.00 $300.00   7

Musical Clown, New Adventures of Clown, 1960s, T–N Co., 9" tall, three actions

$150.00 $300.00   6

Musical Comic Jumping Jeep, Alps Co., 12" long, five actions

$60.00 $120.00   4

Musical Dancing Sweethearts, 1950s, K–O Co., 10" tall, minor toy

$200.00 $400.00   9

Musical Drummer Robot, 1950s, T–N Co., 8¼" tall, three actions

$4,000.00 $8,000.00+   10

Musical Ice Cream Truck, 1960s, Bandai Co., 10½" long, five actions

$150.00 $300.00   6

Musical Jackal, 1950s, Linemar Co., 10" tall, six actions

$500.00 $1,000.00+   10

Musical Jolly Chimp, 1960s, C–K Co., 10½" high, five actions, two cycles

$50.00 $100.00   1

Musical Marching Bear, 1950s, Alps Co., four actions, 11" tall, includes detachable tin horn

$300.00 $600.00   7

Musical Melody Mixer, 1970s, Taiyo Kogyo Co., 10½" long, four actions, includes extra musical bars, mostly plastic
    $40.00 $80.00   3

Musical Showboat, 1960s, Gakken Toy Co., 13" long, minor toy, includes two plastic detachable smokestacks
    $125.00   **$250.00**   **5**

Musical Toy Soundwagon, 1960s, Tamco Co., Ltd., 4½" long, minor toy
    $50.00 $100.00   4

Musical Vegetable Truck, 1960s, Bandai Co., 10½" long, five actions
    $150.00 $300.00   6

Mystery Action Plane, XF–160, with flashing lights, 1950s, T–N Co., 11" long, 11" wingspan, four actions
    $150.00 $300.00   5

Mystery Action Satellite, 1960s, Cragstan Co., 9" long, three actions, includes styro saucer
    $80.00 $160.00   5

Mystery Fire Chief Car No. 81, 1950s, Sanshin Co., 9¼" long, three actions
    $100.00 $200.00   4

Mystery Mike—The Minstrel Man, 1960s, Bell Products Co., 14" tall, minor toy, microphone activated
    $70.00 $140.00   7

Mystery Moon Man, see Chief Robot Man

Mystery Plane, 1950s, T–N Co., four actions, 10" long, 10½" wingspan
    $120.00 $240.00   5

Mystery Police Car, 1960s, T–N Co., 9¾" long, 6" wide, 4" high, three actions
    $100.00 $200.00   4

Mystery Police Car, 1950s, Sanshin Co., 9½" long, three actions, Mercedes 300 SL
    $110.00 $220.00   5

Mystery Space Explorer Tank, 1950s, AHI Co., 8" long, five actions, includes detachable antenna
    $200.00 $400.00   8

NAR Television Truck, see Television Truck With Movable Cameramen and Cameras

Naughty Dog and Buzzing Bee, M-T Co., 10" long, four actions
    $60.00   **$120.00**   **4**

Neptune Tugboat, 1950s, M-T Co., 15" long, 7" high, four actions
    $90.00   **$180.00**   **2**

New Astronaut Robot, 1970s, S–H Co., 9½" tall, six actions
    $80.00 $160.00   2

New Bell Ringer Choo Choo Locomotive, 1960s, M-T Co., 10" long, three actions

$50.00 $100.00   3

New Flip-Flap Flyer, 1960s, Taiwan, 14" high assembled, nine piece set, mostly plastic

$50.00 $100.00   8

New Flying Saucer With Space Pilot, 1960s, KO Co., 7½" diameter, five actions, includes conical spring antenna, NASA logo on fin

$120.00 $240.00   6

New Impy Motorboat, 1950s, International Mosels Products, 11½" long, minor toy, (mostly wood)

$60.00 $120.00   6

New Jumbo The Bubble Blowing Elephant, see Jumbo The Bubble Blowing Elephant

New Silver Mountain Express, 1960s, M-T Co., 16" long, three actions

$40.00 $80.00   2

New Sky Robot, 1960s, S–H Co., 8¾" tall, three actions, mostly plastic

$60.00 $120.00   2

New Space Capsule, 1960s, S–H Co., six actions, 9" long

$120.00   **$240.00**   **3**

New Space Explorer, 1960s, S–H Co., 11½" tall, five actions

$120.00 $240.00   5

Newbuggy Crazy Car, M-T Co., 10" long, minor toy

$50.00 $100.00   4

News Service Car–World News, TPS Co., 9½" long, three actions, resembles Porsche 911

$200.00 $400.00   7

Noel Lantern, lantern toy, 1950s, M–S Co., 5¾" high, minor toy, glass wreath

$60.00   **$120.00**   **9**

Non-Stop Boat, 1950s, Asahi Toy Co., 10½" long, three actions

$90.00 $180.00   7

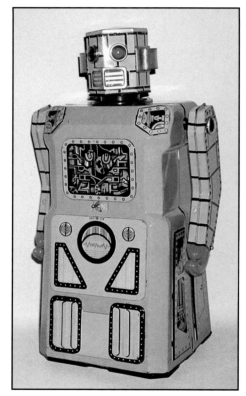

Non-Stop Robot, 1950s, M-T Co., 15" tall, four actions, a.k.a. Lavender Robot

$2,000.00   **$4,000.00+**   **6**

Northwest DC-6 Airliner, 1950s, A.T.C. Co., 15½" long, 19¼" wingspan, seven actions with sequential spinning propellors

$200.00 $400.00   8

Nutty Mad Indian, 1960s, Marx, 12" tall, four actions

$90.00 $180.00   1

Nutty Mad's Car, Drincar, 1960s, Marx Co., 9¼" long, three actions

$175.00 $350.00   4

Nutty Nibs, 1950s, Linemar, 11½" tall, includes litho bowl of nuts and steel ball, minor toy

550.00 $1,100.00   7

007 Unmarked Secret Agent's Car, 1960s, Spesco Co., Joy Toy, 14" long, five actions

$200.00 $400.00   5

Ol' MacDonald's Farm Truck, 1960s, Frankonia, four actions, includes plastic pig, cow, and chicken

$100.00 $200.00   4

Ol' Sleepy Head Rip, 1950s, Y Co., 9" long, seven actions

$150.00 $300.00   6

Old Fashioned Car, 1950s, S–H Co., 10" long, four actions

$50.00 $100.00   1

Old Fashioned Fire Engine, 1950s, M-T Co., four actions, 12½" long

$120.00 $240.00   4

Old Fashioned Fire Engine Carrying Free Flying Ball, 1950s, M-T Co., 10½" long, four actions, includes celluloid ball

$100.00 $200.00   6

Old Fashioned Hot Rod With Driver, 1960s, Bandai Co., 6½" long, four actions

$120.00 $240.00   6

Old Fashioned Telephone Bear, (?) 1950s, M-T Co., 9½" high, four actions

$100.00 $200.00   4

Old Ford Touring Car, 1950s, Z Co., 10" long, four actions

$40.00 $80.00   2

Old Time Automobile, 1950s, Y Co., 8¾" long, three actions, includes detachable tin litho driver and steering wheel

$80.00 $160.00   2

Old Timer Car, 1950s, Cragstan Co., 9" long, three actions

$90.00 $180.00   2

Old Timer Locomotive And Tender, 1950s, H.T.C. Co., 6½" long, three actions

$40.00 $80.00   6

Old Timer Taxi, 1960s, Alps Co., 10" long, five actions

$60.00 $120.00   4

Oldtimer Automoball, 1950s, M-T Co., 10" long, three actions, includes celluloid ball

$90.00 $180.00   5

Oldtimer Locomotive and Tender, 1950s, Mikuni Co., 6½" long, three actions

$60.00	$120.00	8

Oldtimer Sunday Driver, 1960s, Daiya Co., 9" long, four actions

$100.00	$200.00	4

Open Sleigh, 1950s, M-T Co., 16" long, four actions, w/Eskimo

$350.00	**$700.00**	**8**

Overland Choo Choo Express Locomotive, 1950s, M-T Co., 14" long, minor toy

$30.00	$60.00	1

Overland Express #3648, 1960s, M-T Co., 11" long, three actions

$40.00	$80.00	2

Overland Express Locomotive #3140, 1950s, M-T Co., 14" long, minor toy, Indian head logo

$40.00	$80.00	2

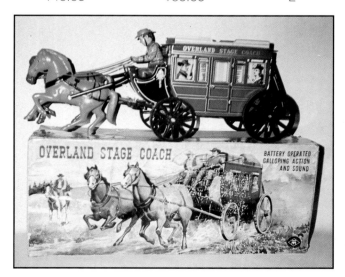

Overland Stage Coach, 1950s, M-T Co., 18" long, four actions, two plastic horses

$150.00	**$300.00**	**6**

P-51 Mustang Shooting Fighter Plane, 1950s, T–N Co., 9" long, 9" wingspan, minor toy

$90.00	$180.00	4

Pacific Piping Express Locomotive, 1960s, Kanto Toy Co., 14" long, four actions

$40.00	$80.00	1

Pan Am Jet Cockpit, 1960s, Remco Co., 17¼" long, 9¾" high, three actions, includes two headsets, flight log, landing check list

$100.00	$300.00	8

Pan Am Sky Taxi–Helicopter, 1960s, Haji Co., 11" long, three actions

$90.00	$180.00	3

Pan American World Airways 'Seven Seas' DC-7, 1950s, T–N Co., 15" long, 19" wingspan, five actions

$140.00	**$280.00**	**4**

Panda Bear, 1970s, M-T Co., Masudaya Co., 10" long, four actions, mostly plastic

$30.00	$60.00	2

Papa Bear–Reading & Drinking in his Old Rocking Chair, 1950s, M-T Co., 10" high, four actions

$150.00	$300.00	6

Passenger Bus, 1950s, Y Co., 16" long, four actions

$230.00	**$460.00**	**7**

Pat O'Neill, 1960s, T–N Co., 12" tall, standing, six actions
     $150.00 $300.00   6

Pat the Dog, 1950s, NGS Co., 9½" long, five actions, two cycles
     $30.00 $60.00   2

Pat the Roaring Elephant, 1950s, Y Co., 9" long with attached baby elephant, four actions
     $150.00 $300.00   6

Patrol Auto-Tricycle, 1960s, T–N Co., 19" long, 7½" high, four actions
     $200.00   **$400.00**   **4**

Patrol Helicopter, Bell–12", 1960s, M-T Co., 17" long, four actions
     $80.00 $160.00   4

Patrol Helicopter No. 7, 1960s, Bandai Co., 11" long, four actions
     $70.00 $140.00   4

P.D. No. 5–Police Patrol Car, Buick, 1960s, Asakusa Toy Co., 11½" long, three actions
     $80.00 $160.00   4

Pee Pee Puppy, 1960s, T–N Co., 9" long, five actions, includes plastic water bottle
     $70.00   **$140.00**   **2**

Penguin on Tricycle, see Cyclist Penguin

Pepi–Tumbling Monkey, 1960s, Yanoman Toy Co., 9½" high, minor toy
     $40.00 $80.00   2

Peppermint Twist Doll, 1950s, Haji Co., 12" tall, minor toy
     $150.00 $300.00   5

Peppy Puppy with Bone, 1950s, Y Co., 8" long, 6½" high, seven actions, two cycles, includes tin litho bone
     $50.00 $100.00   3

Perky Pup, 1960s, Alps Co., 8½" high, three actions
     $50.00 $100.00   2

Pet Turtle, 1960s, Alps Co., 7" long, four actions, two cycles
     $70.00 $140.00   3

Pete the Space Man, 1960s, Bandai Co., 5" tall, minor action, Walking Mate Series
     $60.00 $120.00   4

Pete The Talking Parrot, 1950s, T–N Co., 18" high, six actions, includes instruction tag
     $200.00   **$400.00**   **3**

Peter the Drumming Rabbit, 1950s, Alps Co., VIA–Cragstan, 13" tall, five actions
     $150.00 $300.00   3

Peter The Jolly Drumming Bunny, 1950s, Alps co., 9½" high, six actions, includes detachable drum set and cymbals
$100.00 $200.00   6

Phantom Raider, 1950s, Ideal Toy Co., 34" long extended, four actions, mostly plastic, includes rockets, depth charges, and torpedoes, mostly plastic
$90.00 $180.00   6

Phillips '66' Power Yacht, 1950s, unmarked, 18" long, includes plastic parts for yacht and dock, minor toy, mostly plastic
$70.00 $140.00   2

Photoing On Car, 1970s, China, 12" long, six actions
$20.00   **$40.00**   **1**

Pick-up Truck, T–N Co., 10" long, four actions
$100.00 $200.00   4

Picnic Bear, 1950s, with Coke, Pepsi, or generic logo, Alps Co., 10" high, five actions
$90.00   **$180.00**   **2**

Picnic Bunny, 1950s, Alps Co., 10" tall, four actions
$100.00 $200.00   2

Picnic Monkey, 1950s, Alps Co., 10" high, four actions
$70.00 $140.00   4

Pilot Electro Boat, 1950s, T–N Co., 9½" long, minor toy
$60.00 $100.00   8

Picnic Poodle, 1950s, STS Co., 7"l, 7"h, four actions, two cycles
$40.00 $80.00   2

Pierrot–Monkey Cycle, 1950s, M-T Co., 8" long, 10½" high, five actions
$300.00   **$600.00**   **7**

Piggy Barbecue, 1950s, Y Co., 9½" tall, five actions, includes chef's hat and tin litho fried egg
$150.00 $300.00   5

Piggy Cook, 1950s, Y Co., 9½" tall, 4"x6" base, five actions, includes chef's hat and tin litho fried egg
$140.00   **$280.00**   **2**

Pinkee The Farmer, farm truck with pigs, 1950s, T–N Co., 9½" long, seven actions
$110.00 $220.00   4

Pinky the Juggling Clown, 1950s, Rock Valley Toy Co., Via, 10¼" tall, five actions, includes tin litho propeller, ball on nose
$200.00 $400.00   5

Pinocchio, (Playing London Bridge), 1962, T–N, Rosko, 10" tall, three actions, includes xylophone
$150.00 $300.00   2

Pioneer Covered Wagon, 1960s, Ichida Co., 14½" long, four actions, includes detachable canopy and driver
$140.00 $280.00   6

Pioneer Spirit–Prairie Schooner With Flashing Lights, 1950s, Alps Co., 12" long, minor toy

    $90.00 $180.00   8

Pipie the Whale, 1950s, Alps Co., 12" long, minor toy

    $150.00 $300.00   7

Pirate Ship, 1950s, M-T Co., 13" long, four actions

    $250.00 $500.00   7

Pistol Pete, 1950s, Marusan Co., 5 actions, 10¼" high, includes tin hat

    $250.00   **$500.00**   **6**

Piston Action Bulldozer, 1960s, Linemar Co., 7½" long, five actions, two cycles

    $90.00 $180.00   3

Piston Action Robot, 1950s, T–N Co., 8¼" tall, three actions, resembles Robbie

    $900.00   **$1,800.00**   **10**

Piston Head Robot, 1960s, S–H Co., 10" tall, three actions

    $200.00 $400.00   7

Piston Race Car, 1970s, M-T Co., 9" long, three actions, with Mickey Mouse or Donald Duck

    $90.00 $180.00   5

Piston Robot, 1960s, S–H Co., 10½" tall, four actions

    $110.00 $220.00   5

Piston Tractor, 1950s, T–N Co., 9" long, four actions, includes detachable tin driver

    $110.00 $220.00   7

Plane, KLM Strato-Cruiser, 1950s, T–N Co., 11¼" long, 14" wingspan, three actions

    $150.00 $300.00   5

Planet Explorer, 1950s, S–H Co., 9" long, four actions

    $150.00 $300.00   5

Planet Explorer, 1960s, M-T Co., 9" long, five actions, includes plastic antenna

    $100.00 $200.00   5

Planet Robot, 1960s, K-O Co., 8¾" tall, four actions

    $400.00 $800.00   8

Planet Rover, wheeled tank, 1960s, J Co., 9" long, 6½" high, six actions

    $140.00 $280.00   4

Planet 'Y' Space Station, 1960s, T–N Co., 9" dia., three actions

    $140.00 $280.00   5

Playful Pup in Shoe, 1960s, Y Co., 10" long, three actions

    $50.00 $100.00   5

Playful Puppy with Caterpillar, M-T Co., 7⅜" long, 5" high, four actions

    $100.00 $200.00   4

Playland Octopus, 1950s, Alps co., 20" long assembled, eight actions

    $400.00 $800.00   8

Playland Train, 1970s, Gakken Co., 7½" diameter, three actions, mostly plastic with seven figures

    $20.00 $40.00   6

Pleasant Kappa, 1950s, A.T.D. Co., 10" high, four actions

    $500.00 $1,000.00+   10

Pluto, 1960s, Linemar Co., 10" long, five actions

    $200.00 $400.00   8

Polar Bear, 1970s, Alps Co., 8" long, three actions
$75.00 $150.00   5

Police Auto Cycle, 1960s, motorcycle and plastic driver, Bandai Co., 11½" long, five actions, remote control
$200.00 $400.00   3

Police Car, 1950s, S Co., 8½" long, three actions, with driver
$70.00 $140.00   7

Police Command Car, Highway Patrol, 1960s, T–N Co., 11½" long, four actions
$60.00 $120.00   4

Police Convertible, Highway Patrol Car, '63 Chevy, 1960s, Daiya Co., 13¾" long, three actions
$120.00 $240.00   6

Police Jeep, 1950s, T–N Co., 13" long, four actions
$70.00 $140.00   5

Police Motorcycle, 1950s, M-T Co., 11¾" long, seven actions
$180.00 $360.00   4

Police No. 5, Police Car, 1950s, T–N Co., 9½" long, four actions
$90.00 $180.00   2

Police Patrol, 1950s, T–N Co., 9½" long, four actions
$110.00 $220.00   8

Police Patrol Car, 1950s, M-T Co., 10½" long, four actions
$90.00 $180.00   6

Police Patrol Jeep, 1960s, T–N Co., 9¼" long, four actions
$100.00 $200.00   3

Pom Pom Tank, 1950s, S& E Co., 12½" long, four actions
$60.00 $120.00   6

Popcorn Eating Bear, (?), 1950s, M-T Co., 9" high, five actions
$100.00 $200.00   4

Pop Corn Vendor (Duck's Popcorn), 1950s, T–N Co., 7½" long, 6" high, five actions, includes detachable umbrella
$200.00 $400.00   7

Popcorn Vendor, No. 4035, 1960s, S&E Co., 8" high, 7" long, six actions, includes tin litho umbrella
$200.00 $400.00   5

Popcorn Vendor Truck, 1960s, T–N Co., 9" long, three actions
$150.00 $300.00   5

Popeye and Rowboat with Moving Oars, 1950s, Linemar co., three actions, 10" long
$5,000.00   10,000.00+   10

Porsche 911, 1960s, Bandai Co., 10" long, six actions
$60.00 $120.00   4

Porsche with Visible Engine, 1964 Bandai Co., 10" long, three actions
$90.00 $180.00   4

Poverty Pup, bank, 1966, Poynter Products Co., 6" long, 4¼" high, three actions
$50.00 $100.00   1

Power-Cruiser Sail Boat, 1950s, N.B.K. Co., 10" long, minor toy
$80.00 $160.00   8

Power Shovel, 1950s, Alps Co., 15" long, extended, six actions

| $90.00 | $180.00 | 2 |

Pretty Peggy Parrot, 1950s, T–N Co., 11" long, six actions

| $150.00 | $300.00 | 3 |

Prince Charming Irresistible Poodle, 1950s, Y Co., 9" long, two cycles, six actions

| $30.00 | $60.00 | 2 |

Princess the Begging Poodle, 1950s, Alps Co., 9" long, 8" high, five actions

| $40.00 | $80.00 | 1 |

Princess the French Poodle, 1950s, Alps Co., 9" long, 8" high, five actions

| $40.00 | $80.00 | 1 |

Professor Owl, 1950s, Y Co., 8" high, five actions, includes two discs

| **$200.00** | **$400.00** | **7** |

Project Yankee Doodle, 1959, Remco Co., 15" long, six actions, includes plastic missiles, rockets, and accessories

| $60.00 | $120.00 | 1 |

Puffy Morris, 1960s, Y Co., 10" tall, five actions, uses real cigarette

| $100.00 | $200.00 | 5 |

Pumpkin Lantern, lantern toy, 1950s, 5" high, minor toy

| $30.00 | $60.00 | 1 |

Puzzled Puppy, 1950s, M-T Co., 7½" long, 5" high, five actions

| $100.00 | $200.00 | 3 |

Quacking Duckling, 1950s, Linemar Co., 5½" long, three actions

| $60.00 | $120.00 | 6 |

Queen of the Sea, 1950s, M-T Co., 21½" long, four actions, includes detachable antenna and flag

| **$300.00** | **$600.00** | **6** |

RCA–NBC Mobile Color T.V. truck, 1950s, Cragstan Co., 9" long, four actions, includes detachable cameraman

| $300.00 | $600.00 | 6 |

R.R. Line Locomotive, 1950s, Marx, 6½" long, four actions

| $50.00 | $100.00 | 2 |

R-35 Robot, 1950s, M-T Co., 7½" tall, five actions

| $300.00 | $600.00 | 3 |

Rabbits And The Carriage, 1950s, S&E Co., 8" long, six actions

| **$150.00** | **$300.00** | **7** |

Race-A-Kart, 1960s, Marx Co., 10½" long, five actions

| $110.00 | $220.00 | 6 |

Racecar #25, 1950s, Alps Co., 9" long, three actions

| $800.00 | $1,600.00 | 9 |

Racing Motorcycle, 1960s, Daiya Co., 10" long, minor toy
$80.00 $160.00   5

Radar Jeep, 1950s, T–N Co., 11" long, four actions
$150.00 $300.00   5

Radar 'N' Scope, 1960s, M-T Co., 10" high, 7" long, four actions, includes detachable tower and antenna
$90.00 $180.00   6

Radar Robot, 1960s, T–N Co., 8" tall, minor toy
$500.00 $1,000.00+   10

Radar Robot, 1960s, T–N Co., 9" tall, three actions, remote "robot-face" control box
$600.00 $1,200.00   8

Radar Robot, 1970s, S–H Co., 12" tall, five actions
$70.00 $140.00   4

Radar Scope Space Scout, 1960s, S–H Co., three actions, 9¼" tall
$140.00 $280.00   5

Radar Tank, 1950s, M-T Co., 8" long, three actions, includes detachable plastic antenna
$120.00 $240.00   5

Radar Tractor and Robot Driver, 1960s, S–H Co., 7½" long, includes detachable plastic antenna
$250.00 $500.00   6

Radicon Boat, 1950s, M-T Co., 14" long, three actions, includes two detachable antennas and transmitter
$300.00 $600.00   6

Radicon Bus, 1950s, M-T Co., 14" long, three actions, includes two detachable antennas and transmitter
$200.00 $400.00   3

Radicon New Sedan, 1950s, M-T Co., 14" long, three actions, includes two detachable antennas and transmitter
$350.00 $700.00   8

Radicon Robot, 1950s, M-T Co., 15" tall, six actions, includes two detachable antennas and transmitter
$2,000.00 $4,000.00+   10

Radio Rex, 1920s, Elmwood Button Co., 5"x7" dog house, minor toy, includes celluloid dog
$100.00 $200.00   4

Radio Televisione Italiana, Ichiko Co., 1960s, 12" long, three actions
$250.00 $500.00   6

Railroad Hand Car, 1950s, KDP Co., 8" long, minor toy, includes rubber track
$90.00 $180.00   2

Railway Yard–Shuttle Train, 1950s, ATC Co., 8" long, track 28" long, three actions, includes locomotive boxcar and track
$100.00 $200.00   3

Rajah Rey–The Indian Prince, 1960s, T–N Co., 12" tall, six actions
$125.00 $250.00   7

Rambling Lady Bug, 1960s, MT Co., 8" long, minor toy

$60.00   **$120.00**   **2**

Ranger Jeep, 1950s, T-N Co., 11" long, four actions

$120.00 $140.00   8

Ranger Robot, see Super Space Commander

Ray Gun, machine gun, 1950s, T-N Co., 17½" long, three actions, includes tripod

$50.00 $100.00   3

Reading Bear, see Wee Little Baby Bear

Red Express #4292 Locomotive, 1950s, M-T co., 11¼" long, four actions

$40.00 $80.00   2

Rembrandt the Monkey Artist, 1950s, Alps Co., 8" high, five actions

$200.00   **$400.00**   **7**

Remote Control Runner Boat, 1950s, M–H–M Co., 11" long, minor toy

$60.00 $120.00   6

Rendezvous 7.8-Space Station, 1960s, Y Co., 15" long extended, five actions, includes detachable tin rocket

$1,500.00 $3,000.00+   10

Reversible Diesel Electric Tractor, 1950s, Marx Co., minor toy

$60.00 $120.00   4

Ricki–The Begging Poodle, 1950s, Rock Valley Toys (VIA), 9" long, 8" high, five actions

$30.00 $60.00   1

River Boat, 1950s, Marusan Co., 12¾" long, three actions, includes detachable tin smokestack

$130.00   **$260.00**   **3**

River Queen Sidewheeler, 1950s, M-T Co., 13½" long, three actions

$140.00 $280.00   3

River Steam Boat, 1950s, M-T Co., 13" long, three actions, includes detachable plastic smokestack

$100.00 $200.00   4

Road Construction Roller, 1950s, Daiya Co., 8½" long, four actions

$60.00 $120.00   3

Road Grader, 1960s, T–N Co., 12" long, three actions

$50.00 $100.00   2

Road Roller, 1950s, M-T Co., 9" long, four actions

$60.00 $120.00   2

Roaring Gorilla, see Gorilla

Roaring Gorilla Shooting Gallery, 1950s, M-T Co., 9½" tall, three actions, includes fold-out target box, tin gun, plastic darts

$200.00	**$400.00**	**4**

Roarin' Jungle Lion, 1950s, Marx Co., 16" long nose to tail tip, four actions, two cycles

$140.00	$280.00	5

Roaring Lion, 1950s, T–N Co., 11" long, six actions, two cycles

$100.00	**$200.00**	**5**

Robby Robot, see Mechanized Robot

Robby Space Patrol, 1950s, T–N Co., 12½" long, five actions, original

$2,000.00	$4,000.00+	10

Robert the Robot, 1950s, Ideal Toy Co., 14" tall, three actions, B.O. light only

$120.00	**$240.00**	**1**

Robert the Robot on his Mechanical Bulldozer, 1950s, Ideal Toy Co., 9" long, four actions, B.O. light only

$300.00	**$600.00**	**8**

Robot, 1960s, Y Co., 11" tall, four actions, a.k.a. Directional Robot

$600.00	$1,200.00	7

Robot Bulldozer, 1950s, United Pioneer Co., 1950s, 8" long, four actions

$400.00	$800.00	8

Robot Machine 7021–Kinsman, 1985, TPS by Dah Yang Toy Co., 13" high assembled, four actions, mostly plastic, includes three robots, sign, and two tracks
$90.00 $180.00 6

Robot Operated Bulldozer With Automatic Shovel Action, 1950s, K-O Co., 7" long, five actions
$600.00 $1,200.00 8

Robot–Revolving & Flashing, 1950s, Alps Co., 9½" tall, remote control, three actions a.k.a Door Robot
$1,000.00 $2,000.00+ 10

Robot–Shoot Him, 1950s, M-T Co.m, 15" tall, four actions, a.k.a Target Robot, includes tin gun and rubber tipped darts
$2,000.00 $4,000.00+ 9

Robot 2500, 1970s, Durham Industries, 10½" tall, four actions
$60.00 $120.00 2

Robot With Flashing Lighted Eyes and Moving Arms, 1950s, Linemar Co., 6" tall, four actions, a.k.a. Gold Robot
$2,000.00 $4,000.00+ 9

Robot With Lighted Eyes and Smoke And Lighted Lantern, 1950s, Linemar Co., 7¾" tall, four actions, a.k.a. Lantern Robot
$2,000.00 $4,000.00+ 10

Robo Tank (Mini), 1960s, T–N Co., 5" tall, five actions
$150.00 $300.00 5

Robotank TR-2, 1950s, T–N Co., 5" high, four actions
$140.00 $280.00 5

Robotank Z Space Robot, 1960s, T–N Co., 10¼" high, five actions
$300.00 $600.00 6

Robotrack Bulldozer, 1960s, Linemar Co., 9" long, three actions
$350.00 $700.00 7

Rock 'N' Roll Hotrod, see Hot Rod

Rock 'N' Roll Monkey, 1950s, Rosko Co., 13" tall, five actions, includes plastic hat, three variations
$160.00 $320.00 2

Rocket Express, Rocket Ship Monorail, 1950s, Linemar Co., three actions, 10" long, 20 piece rail and girder set
$100.00 $200.00 5

Rocket Launching Pad, 1950s, Y Co., 8½" high, five actions, includes tin litho satellite and rocket
$160.00 $320.00 6

Rocking Santa, 1950s, Alps Co., 10" high, four actions
$300.00 $600.00 8

Rocky, 1960s, Linemar Co., 3" diameter, minor toy, Flintstone knock-off
$100.00 $200.00 3

Rocky The Beer Man, 1970s, Hong Kong, 10" tall, four actions
$40.00 $80.00 3

Rocky—Robotron—the Mechanical Maniac, 1970, Topper Corp., Japan, 8" tall, three actions, includes three plastic darts
$70.00 $140.00   5

Roll-Over Rover, 1970s, Mego Co., 9" long, three actions
$40.00 $80.00   2

Roller Skater, 1950s, Alps Co., minor toy, 12" tall
$90.00 $180.00   3

Rollerskating Clown, 1950s, TPS Co., 6" tall, minor toy
$500.00 $1,000.00+   10

ROM—The Space Knight, 1970s, Parker Bros. Co., 13" tall, minor toy
$50.00 $100.00   1

Romance Car M-841, 1950s, M Co., 8" long, three actions
$140.00 $280.00   7

Root Beer Counter, 1960s, K Co., 8" long, 8" high, three actions, includes plastic barrel, glasses and tin tray
$100.00 $200.00   5

Rosemarie Cabin Cruiser, 1950s, Marusan Co., 13½" long, minor toy
$120.00 $240.00   7

Rosko Robot, see Astronaut (with Walkie Talkie)

Rotate-O-Matic Super Astronaut, 1960s, S–H Co., 11½" tall, six actions, two cycles
$100.00 $200.00   1

Rotate-O-Matic Super Giant Robot, S–H Co., 16" tall, six actions
$100.00 $200.00   2

Rotator Robot, 1960s, S–H Co., 12" tall, six actions
$130.00 $260.00   3

Roto-Robot, 1960s, S–H Co., 8½" tall, five actions, gray or gold colors
$100.00 $200.00   5

Rover the Poodle Bell Ringer, 1960s, Alps Co., 10½" tall, three actions, two cycles
$60.00 $120.00   1

Roy Rogers Ranch Lantern, lantern toy, 1950s, Ohio Art, 12" tall, extended, minor toy
$80.00 $160.00   2

Roy Rogers Western Telephone, Ideal Co., 1950s, three actions, 9" high
$90.00 $180.00   4

Royal Cub in Buggy, 1950s, S&E Co., 8" long, 8" high, six actions
$150.00 $300.00   2

Rudy the Robot, 1968, Remco Co., 16¼" tall, four actions

$110.00 $220.00   2

S.S. Moby Dick—Whaling Ship, 1950s, Rico Co., 15½" long, three actions

$300.00 $600.00   9

SSN-571 Submarine, Nautilus, 1950s, Marusan Co., 16" long with rudder extended, minor toy

$120.00   **$240.00**   **5**

SSN-571 Submarine, Skate, 1950s, Marusan Co., 16" long with rudder extended, minor toy

$120.00 $240.00   5

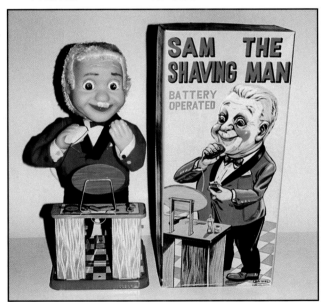

Sam the Shaving Man, 1960s, Plaything Toy Co., 11½" tall, seven actions, includes metal mirror

$150.00   **$300.00**   **6**

Sammy Wong—The Tea Totaler, 1950s, T–N Co., 10" tall, four actions

$160.00 $320.00   7

Sandy Snooper With Butterfly, 1960s, Alps Co., 8½" long, 8½" high, four actions

$40.00 $80.00   4

Santa Bank, 1960, HTC Co., (Trim a Tree), 11" high, four actions

$150.00   **$300.00**   **2**

Santa Claus, bell ringer, 1950s, Alps Co., 10" tall, three actions

$60.00 $120.00   6

Santa Claus, No. M-750 (Sitting on House), 1950s, H.T.C. Co., 8" high, four actions

$100.00 $200.00   1

Santa Claus—Bellringer, 1950s, Santa Creations Co., 13" tall, five actions

$90.00   **$180.00**   **1**

Santa Claus Lantern, lantern toy, 1950s, unmarked, 6½" high, minor toy

$70.00 $140.00   8

Santa Claus on Handcar, 19650s, M-T Co., 10" high, three actions

$120.00 $240.00   2

Santa Fe Diesel, Battery Cable Train With Headlight, 1950s, T-N Co., 13½" long, two piece hookup, minor toy

$80.00 $160.00   5

Santa in Rocker, see Merry Christmas

Santa Claus on Reindeer Sleigh, 1950s, M-T Co., 17" long, five actions

$400.00 $800.00   8

Santa Claus on Scooter, 1950s, M-T Co., 10" high, four actions
$120.00 $240.00   2

Santa Claus With Blinking Wand, (?), 1950s, Santa Creations, 13" tall, six actions
$200.00 $400.00   8

Santa Copter, 1950s M-T Co., 8½" long, three actions
$70.00 $240.00   1

Santa Claus Phone Bank, 1950s, S&E Co., 7 actions, 8" high, includes remote 4¾" high payphone
$400.00 $800.00   9

Santa Face Globe Christmas Lantern, lantern toy, 1950s, Amico Co., 5¾" high, minor toy
$50.00 $100.00   6

Santa the Bellringer, 1950s, Chase Import Co., 7" high, electro-magnet activated by a blinker bulb, minor toy

$100.00 $150.00   6

Satellite In Orbit, 1950s, S–H Co., 9" high, three actions, includes styrofoam ball
$200.00 $400.00   8

Satellite Intercepter Target Set, 1950s, Linemar Co., two piece set with 6½" long gun-telescope, 5" high blower, two plastic darts, and styro ball, minor toy
$150.00 $300.00   4

Satellite Target Game, 1960s, S-H Co., 8" high, 10½" wide, includes celluloid ball and special gun, minor toy
$100.00 $200.00   1

Satellite X-107, with floating ball, 1960s, M-T Co., 8" diameter, five actions, includes styrofoam ball
$300.00 $600.00   7

Satellite X-107, *see Cragstan Mystery Action Satellite*

Saxophone Playing Monkey, 1950s, Alps Co., 9½" high, four actions

$250.00　　　　　**$500.00**　　　　　**8**

School Bus, 1950s, Cragstan, 20½" long, minor toy
　　$70.00　　　　　$140.00　　　　　4

Schuco Elektro #5511/2, motorboat, 1950s, Schuco Co., 8½" long, minor toy, mostly plastic with detachable driver
　　$110.00　　　　　$220.00　　　　　8

Schuco Samara II–Chris Craft, motorboat, 1950s, Schuco Co., 15" long, minor toy, mostly plastic
　　$70.00　　　　　$140.00　　　　　8

Sea Bear #7 Racing Boat, 1950s, Bandai Co., 10" long, minor toy
　　$60.00　　　　　$120.00　　　　　4

Searchlight Jeep, 1950s, T-N Co., 7¾" long, three actions
　　$90.00　　　　　$180.00　　　　　6

Searchlight Jeep with Artillery, 1950s, T-N Co., Electro Toy, 17" long, Jeep 7½" long, artillery 8½" long, four actions
　　$150.00　　　　　$300.00　　　　　7

Searchlight Truck, 1950s, M-T Co., 11" long, three actions
　　$160.00　　　　　$320.00　　　　　5

Seascape Tugboat, 1950s, Marx Co., 6½" long, three actions
　　$50.00　　　　　$100.00　　　　　5

Secret Service Action Car, Green Hornet motif, 1960s, ASC Co., 11" long, four actions
　　$400.00　　　　　$800.00+　　　　　10

Secret Weapon Space Scout Astronaut, 1960s, S-H Co., 9" tall, six actions
　　$350.00　　　　　$700.00　　　　　9

Serpent Charmer, 1950s, Linemar Co., 7" high, four actions
　　$500.00　　　　　$1,000.00+　　　　　9

Sewing Machine, 1960s, WACO CO., 6" long, minor toy
　　$30.00　　　　　$60.00　　　　　4

Shaggy the Friendly Pup, 1960s, Alps Co., 8" long, three actions
　　$40.00　　　　　$80.00　　　　　1

Shaking Classic Car, 1960s, T-N Co., 7" long, four actions
　　$50.00　　　　　$100.00　　　　　1

Shaking Old-Timer Car No. 2511-1, 1960s, T-N Co., 9" long, four actions, includes plastic driver
　　$60.00　　　　　$120.00　　　　　1

Shark-U-Control Racing Car, 1961, Remco Ind. Inc., 19" long, all plastic, minor toy
　　$80.00　　　　　**$160.00**　　　　　**1**

Sheriff Car, 1950s, T-N Co., 10" long, four actions
　　$80.00　　　　　$160.00　　　　　2

Sheriff Sam The Crazy Cowboy, 1960s, Marx Co., England, 6" long, minor toy, mostly plastic
　　$60.00　　　　　$120.00　　　　　7

Shoe-Shaking Dog, 1950s, M-T Co., 8" long, 6" tall, five actions
　　$60.00　　　　　$120.00　　　　　4

Shoe Shine Bear, 1950s, T-N Co., 9" tall, five actions
　　$130.00　　　　　$260.00　　　　　2

Shoe Shine Joe, 1950s, T-N Co., 11" high, six actions, two variations

      $140.00 $280.00   **3**

Shoe Shine Monkey, 1950s, T-N Co., 9" high, five actions

      $140.00 $280.00   3

Shooting Bear, 1950s, SAN Co., 10" tall, six actions

      $160.00 $320.00   7

Shooting Gorilla, 1950s, M-T Co., 12" high, four actions, includes gun and darts

      $160.00 $320.00   4

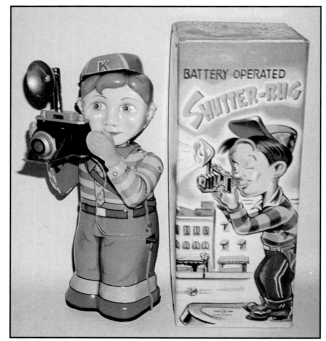

Shutterbug, photographer, 1950s, T-N Co., tall, five actions

      $400.00   **$800.00**   **6**

Shuttling Freight Train, 1950s, Cragstan Co., six actions, 51" long assembled, includes locomotive, lumber car, four piece track, platform, logs

      $110.00 $220.00   5

Shuttling Train and Freight Yard, 1950s, Alps Co., 11" long, track 51" long, four actions, includes locomotive, baggage car, two platforms, litho luggage

      $120.00 $240.00   **5**

Sight Seeing Bus, 1960s, Bandai Co., 14½" long, four actions

      $100.00 $200.00   5

Sight Seeing Bus, 1950s, Yonezawa Co., 9" long, minor toy

      $140.00 $280.00   5

Sight-Seeing Planes, 1950s, M-T Co., 11½" high, three actions, includes crossbar and two tin airplanes

      $200.00 $400.00   9

Sight-Seeing Sound Bus, 1950s, M-T Co., 14¼" long, minor toy

      $110.00 $220.00   6

Sikorsky Rescue Army Helicopter, 1950s, Alps Co., 11" long, four actions

      $90.00 $180.00   5

Silver Bell Choo Choo, 1950s, Kanto Co., 12" long, three actions

      $40.00 $80.00   1

Silver Mariner Cargo Liner, 1950s, Bandai Co., 15" long, five actions, includes cargo of tanks

    $200.00 $400.00   6

Silver Mountain Express Locomotive, 1960s, M-T Co., four actions, 15¾" long

    $40.00 $80.00   1

Silver Mountain Locomotive, 1950s, M-T Co., 16" long, three actions

    $40.00 $80.00   1

Silver Ray Secret Weapon Space Scout, 1960s, S-H Co., 9" tall, six actions

    $750.00 $1,500.00+   10

Silver Skipper Aluminum Streamlined Boat, 1950s, Reeves Products Co., 14½" long with motor, minor toy

    $100.00   **$200.00**   **7**

Silver Streak Locomotive No. 6682, 1950s, M-T Co., 16" long, four actions

    $40.00 $80.00   1

Singing Bird In Cage, 1950s, T-N Co., 9" high, 4" x 6" rectangular base, four actions

    $100.00   **$200.00**   **4**

Singing Circus, 1960s, Tomy Co., 10" long, four actions, includes detachable giraffe head

    $70.00 $140.00   6

Siren Fire Car, 1950s, M-T Co., 9" long, four actions

    $130.00 $260.00   4

Siren Patrol Car, 1960s, M-T Co., four actions, 12½" long

    $90.00 $180.00   4

Siren Patrol Motorcycle, 1960s, M-T Co., 12" long, three actions

    $200.00 $400.00   6

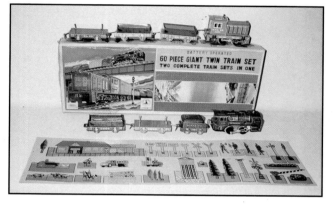

60 Piece Giant Twin Train Set, 1950s, Haji Co., 16" long diesel train, 15" long steam train, two complete trains with locomotives, three cars and cardboard punchouts, minor toy

    $100.00   **$200.00**   **8**

Skating Circus Clown, 1950s, TPS Co., 6" tall, minor toy

    $500.00 $1,000.00+   10

Ski Lift, 1950s, Bandai Co., 6" long, 5" high, minor toy

    $60.00 $120.00   4

Skiing Santa, 1960s, M-T Co., 12" tall, four actions, includes tin skis

    $150.00 $300.00   5

Skipping Monkey, 1960s, T-N Co., 9½" tall, minor toy

    $40.00 $80.00   3

Skull Lantern, lantern toy, 1950s, Amico Co., minor toy

    $50.00 $100.00   3

Sky-Guard Jet With Lighted Dome, 1950s, Showa Co., 12" long, 10" wingspan, four actions, marked U.S.A.F.

    $240.00 $480.00   8

Sky Patrol Space Cruiser, 1950s, T-N Co., 13" long, five actions

    $150.00 $300.00   5

Sky Patrol Flying Saucer, 1950s, K-O Co., 7½" diameter, seven actions, includes detachable antenna

    $100.00 $200.00   3

Sky Robot, 1960s, S-H Co., 8¾" tall, three actions

    $60.00 $120.00   1

Sky Sweeper, 1960s, Ideal Toy Co., 25" long, three actions, includes six plastic darts

    $70.00 $140.00   5

Sky Taxi—Pan Am—Boeing Vertol 107, 1970s, Haji Co., 12¾" long, three actions, includes two detachable rotors

    $120.00 $240.00   5

Skyliner Sports Car, 1950s, T-N Co., 9" long, four actions

    $110.00 $220.00   6

Slalom Game, 1960s T-N Co., 15¼" long, includes plastic skier, minor toy

    $100.00   **$200.00**   **7**

Sleeping Baby Bear, 1950s, Linemar, 9" long, six actions, includes detachable alarm clock

    $240.00 $480.00   2

Sleepy Pup, 1960s, Alps Co., 12" long nose tip to tail tip, five actions

    $40.00   **$80.00**   **4**

Slurpy Pup, 1960s, T-N Co., 6½" long, 4" high, four actions

    $50.00   **$100.00**   **2**

Smarty Bird, 1964, Ideal Toy Co., 16" tall, 19" long, four actions

    $60.00 $120.00   7

Smilex Deluxe Coffee Set, 1950s, Y Co., 12" high assembled, includes four sets of plastic cups, saucers and spoons, minor toy

    $60.00 $120.00   3

Smokey Bear Jeep, 1950s, M-T Co., 10" long, four actions

    $220.00 $440.00   7

Smokey Bill on Old Fashioned Car, 1960s, T-N Co., 9" long, four actions

    $120.00 $240.00   5

Smoking And Shoe Shining Panda Bear, 1950s, Alps Co., 10½" high

    $120.00 $240.00   5

Smoking Bulldozer, 1960s, Daiya Co., 9½" long, three actions, includes detachable head

    $110.00 $220.00   6

Smoking Bulldozer, 1960s, WKC Co., 9" long, four actions

$90.00 $180.00   5

Smoking Bunny, 1950s, SAN Co., 10½" tall, four actions
$100.00 $200.00   6

Smoking Engine Robot, 1970s, S-H Co., 10½" tall, five actions

$50.00 $100.00   2

Smoking Elephant, 1950s, Marusan Co., 8¾" tall, four actions

$130.00 $260.00   5

Smoking Spaceman, 1950s, Linemar Co., 12" tall, six actions, original
$800.00   **$1,600.00**   **8**

Smoking U.S.A.F. Jet, see Jet Plane with Smoking & Tail Light

Smoking Volkswagen, 1960s, Aoshin Co., 10½" long, four actions

$60.00 $120.00   2

Smoking Grandpa in Rocking Chair, 1950s, SAN Co., 8" tall, four actions, Type I, eyes open
$150.00   **$300.00**   **1**

Smoking Grandpa in Rocking Chair, 1950s, SAN Co., 8" tall, four actions, Type II, eyes closed
$160.00 $320.00   2

Smoking Jet Plane, 1950s, T-N Co., 12" long, 11" wingspan, four actions

$150.00 $300.00   6

Smoking Papa Bear, SAN Co., 8" tall, four actions
$120.00 $240.00   2

Smoking Pop Locomotive—The General, 1950s, SAN Co., 10¼" long, four actions

$70.00 $140.00   3

Smoking Popeye, 1950s, Linemar, 9" tall, five actions
$800.00 $1,600.00+   9

Smoky Bear, 1950s, SAN Co., 9" tall, four actions, includes detachable tin Pioneer hat
$220.00   **$440.00**   **6**

Smoky Joe—Fancy Mobile, 1960s, T-N Co. 9" long, four actions, smokes, lights, bump and go, noise
$100.00 $200.00   5

Snake Charmer (And Casey the Trained Cobra), 1950s, Linemar Co., 8" high, four actions
$250.00 $500.00   7

Snappy Puppy, 1960s, Alps Co., 8½" long, four actions

| $30.00 | $60.00 | 6 |

Snappy the Happy Bubble Blowing Dragon, 1960s, T-N Co., 30" long, six actions

| $2,000.00 | $4,000.00+ | 10 |

Sneezing Bear, 1950s, Linemar Co., 9" high, five actions

| $200.00 | $400.00 | 4 |

Sniffy Dog, 1970s, Alps Co., 9" long, five actions

| $30.00 | $60.00 | 5 |

Snooper Dog, 1960s, Alps Co., 9" long, four actions

| $40.00 | $80.00 | 3 |

Snoopie the Non-Fall Dog, 1960s, Amico Co., 8" long, three actions

| $50.00 | $100.00 | 2 |

Snoopy Sniffer, 1960s, M-T Co., 8" long, four actions

| $50.00 | $100.00 | 2 |

Snowman With Blinking Nose, lantern toy, 1950s, M-S Co., 6" high, minor toy

| $50.00 | $100.00 | 6 |

Somersaulting Pup With Bark, 1960s, T-N Co., 9" long, two cycles, four actions

| $60.00 | $120.00 | 4 |

Sonic Car Dodge Charger, 1960s, T-N Co., 16" long, three actions, includes whistle

| $200.00 | $400.00 | 6 |

Sonicon Rocket, 1960s, M-T Co., 13½" long, four actions, includes blue plastic whistle and antenna

| $200.00 | $400.00 | 5 |

Sound Bus, 1950s, M-T Co., 14" long, three actions

| $140.00 | $280.00 | 8 |

Space Automatic Pistol, 1950s, Exelo Co., 6½" long, minor toy
$40.00 $80.00   5

Space Beetle No. 2, 1970s, Y Co., 9" long, three actions, mostly plastic, includes detachable antenna
$50.00 $100.00   5

Space Capsule, NASA-Mercury, 1950s, S-H Co., 11" long, four actions, smokes
$200.00 $400.00   8

Space Capsule With Floating Astronaut, 1960s, M-T Co., 10" long, four actions, includes styrofoam saucer and astronaut
$100.00 $200.00   5

Space Capsule–5, 1960s, M-T Co., 10½" long, four actions
$150.00 $300.00   4

Space Car, 1950s, Y Co., 9½" long, six actions, includes styrofoam ball
$500.00 $1,000.00+   8

Space Car, 1960s, M-T Co., 9½" long, four actions
$120.00 $240.00   8

Space Car, SX-10, 1960s, M-T Co., 9½" long, four actions
$100.00 $200.00   6

Space Commander, 1950s, T-N Co., 9" diameter, three actions, a.k.a. Space Station
$150.00 $300.00   7

Space Commander Robot, 1960s, S-H Co., 10" tall, five actions
$1,000.00 $2,000.00+   9

Space Commando–Spaceman, 1960s, M-T Co., 7¾" tall, four actions
$500.00 $1,000.00+   9

Space Commando, Space Station, 1960s, T-N Co., 10" diameter, four actions
$150.00 $300.00   5

Space Conqueror, 1960s, Daiya Co., 14" tall, four actions, similar to Cragstan Astronaut
$400.00 $800.00   5

Space Cruiser With Motor, 1950s, T-N Co., 8½" long, minor toy
$150.00 $300.00   8

Space Exploration Train, 1950s, K-O Co., 21" overall length, four piece set
$400.00 $800.00   8

Space Explorer, 1960s, Ichiko Co., 8½" diameter, four actions
$140.00 $280.00   6

Space Explorer, Astronaut, 1960s, S-H Co., 12" tall, four actions
$100.00 $200.00   5

Space Explorer #1041, 1960s, Yonezawa Co., 7¾" high, extends to 11½" high, six actions
$600.00 $1,200.00+   10

Space Explorer Ship X-7, 1960s, M-T Co., 8" diameter, three actions
$90.00 $180.00   4

Space Fighter Robot, 1970s, S-H Co., 9" tall, six actions
$70.00 $140.00   3

Space Frontier Apollo 12 Rocket, 1960s, K-Y Co., 18" long, six actions
$100.00 $200.00   5

Space Frontier Saturn 5 Rocket, 1960s, K-Y Co., Yoskino Toy Co., 18" long, six actions
$100.00 $200.00   4

Space Giant, 1950s, M-T Co., 12" diameter, three actions
$110.00 $220.00   8

Space Gun, pistol, 1960s, T-N Co., 8" long, minor toy
$70.00 $140.00   6

Space Jet, 1960s, Asahi Toy Co., 7" long, three actions,
Space Patrol on box
$160.00 $320.00   8

Space Orbitestor, 1960s, Asakusa Co., 8" long, three actions, includes plastic satellite orbiter
$90.00 $180.00   3

Space Patrol, vehicle, 1950s, K Co., 9" long, four actions
$130.00 $260.00   5

Space Patrol, vehicle, 1960s, M-T Co., 9½" long, three actions
$100.00 $200.00   5

Space Patrol, vehicle, with double barrel gun, 1960s, S-H Co., 9½" long, three actions
$120.00 $240.00   7

Space Patrol–3, saucer, see Flying Saucer With Space Pilot

Space Patrol 2019, see Flying Saucer

Space Patrol X-16, 1960s, Amico Co., 8" diameter, four actions, includes styro ball
$100.00 $200.00   5

Space Patrol X-17, 1960s, M-T Co., 8" diameter, three actions, includes styro ball
$90.00 $180.00   5

Space Patrol Car, 1950s, T-N Co., four actions, 9½" long, VW car
$800.00 $1,600.00+   9

Space Patrol Car, 1960s, Bandai Co., 12" long, four actions, includes detachable antenna
$400.00 $800.00   8

Space Patrol Car, with Lighting Guns, 1950s, Linemar Co., 9" long, three actions
$600.00 $1,200.00+   9

Space Patrol 'Fire Bird' With Blinking Light, 1950s, M-T Co., 14" long, three actions
$250.00 $500.00   9

Space Patrol–Planet Tank, 1960s, M-T Co., 8" long, three actions, includes detachable plastic antenna
$150.00 $300.00   6

Space Patrol Robot, 1950s, S-H Co., 11" tall, six actions
$140.00 $280.00   5

Space Patrol Rocket, 1970s, M-T Co., 11" long, three actions
$70.00 $140.00   4

Space Patrol–Snoopy, 1960s, M-T Co., 11" long, four actions
$100.00 $200.00   3

Space Patrol Tank, 1950s, Cragstan Co., 9" long, five actions, includes detachable tin jet planes
$150.00 $300.00   6

Space Patrol Tank X-11, 1960s, Yonezawa Co., 8½" long, five actions, includes detachable plastic antenna
$180.00 $360.00   7

Space Patrol With Floating Satellite, 1960s, Amico Co., 7½" diameter, three actions, includes styrofoam ball
$100.00 $200.00   7

Space Pilot Super-Sonic Gun, 1953, Randall Co., England, 9" long, minor toy
$80.00 $160.00   8

Space Pioneer Vehicle, 1960s, M-T Co., 12" long, three actions
$100.00 $300.00   6

Space Refuel Station In Orbital Flight, 1959, WACO Co., 15" high, six actions, includes plastic antenna, tin jet plane, and rocket module
$750.00 $1,500.00+   9

Space Robot–Car, 1950s, Yonezawa Co., 9¼" long, six actions
$1,000.00 $2,000.00+   10

Space Robot Trooper, 1950s, K-O Co., 7½" tall, three actions

　　　$500.00　　　　　$1,000.00+　　　　10

Space Robot With T.V. Camera and Screen, X-70, 1960s, T-N Co., 12" tall, five actions, a.k.a. Tulip Head Robot

　　　$500.00　　　$1,000.00+　　　　6

Space Rocket—Blue Eagle, 1950s, Masuya Toy Co., 15" long tail to probe tip, four actions

　　　$120.00　　　　　$240.00　　　　5

Space Rocket Car With Action Of Jet Propulsion—#75, 1950s, Y Co., 11½" long, three actions

　　　$210.00　　　　　$420.00　　　　9

Space Rocket—Mars 3, 1960s, T-N Co., 15" high, five actions

　　　$100.00　　　　　$200.00　　　　5

Space Rocket—Solar X, 1960s, T-N Co., 15½" tall, five actions

　　　$150.00　　　　　$300.00　　　　3

Space Ruler Machine Gun, 1950s, S-H Co., 22" long, four actions

　　　$100.00　　　　　$200.00　　　　6

Space Saucer—Mercury X-1, 1960s, Y Co., 8" diameter, four actions, includes detachable plastic antenna

　　　$80.00　　　　　$160.00　　　　6

Space Scooter, 1960s, M-T Co., 10½" high, 8" long, three actions

　　　$100.00　　　　　$200.00　　　　1

Space Scooter, Snoopy or Astro-Dog, 1960s, M-T Co., 8" long, three actions

　　　$80.00　　　　　$160.00　　　　2

Space Scout S-17, 1960s, Y Co., 9¾" long, five actions, includes detachable wire-loop antenna

　　　$250.00　　　　　$500.00　　　　**8**

Space Ship, 1950s, I.Y. Co., 9½" diameter, four actions

　　　$180.00　　　　　$360.00　　　　6

Space Ship, 1970s, M-T Co., 9" long, three actions

　　　$90.00　　　　　$180.00　　　　4

Space Ship—Forbidden Planet, 1950s, Childs-Smith Co., England, 5½" diameter, extends to 24", minor toy

　　　$220.00　　　　　$440.00　　　　9

Space Ship X-5, 1970s, M-T Co., 8" diameter, four actions

　　　$60.00　　　　　$120.003

Space Ship X-8, 1960s, Tada Co., 8" long, four actions

　　　$100.00　　　　　$200.00　　　　5

Space Shuttle—Enterprise, 1960s, M-T Co., 10½" long, three actions

　　　$60.00　　　　　$120.00　　　　5

Space Sight Seeing Bus, 1960s, M-T Co., 13" long, three actions

　　　$250.00　　　　　$500.00　　　　9

Space Station, saucer, see Space Commander

Space Station, 1950s, T-N Co.,9" diameter, four actions

　　　$100.00　　　　　$200.00　　　　5

Space Station, 1950s, S-H Co., 11¾" diameter, five actions

　　　$500.00　　　　　$1,000.00　　　　9

Space Station—Man Made Earth Of Space Age, 1959, S-H Co., 14" diameter, five actions, includes detachable plastic antenna

　　　$600.00　　　　　$1,200.00+　　　　8

Space Surveillant X-07, 1960s, M-T Co., 8½" long, five actions
    $150.00 $300.00   7

Space Survey X-09, 1960s, M-T Co., 9" long, five actions
    $150.00 $300.00   7

Space Tank, 1950s, Daiya Co., 8" long, four actions
    $120.00 $240.00   5

Space Tank, 1960s, K-O Co., 6" long, four actions, Robbie Type, original
    $2,000.00 $4,000.00+   10

Space Tank M-18, 1950s, M-T Co., 8½" long, four actions, includes detachable plastic antenna
    $140.00 $280.00   5

Space Tank M-18, 1950s, M-T Co., 8" long, five actions,
    $200.00 $400.00   8

Space Tank M-41, 1950s, M-T Co., 9" long, four actions, includes detachable plastic antenna
    $100.00 $200.00   5

Space Traveling Monkey, 1960s, Yanoman Co., 8½" high, three actions
    $90.00 $180.00   6

Space Trip, 1950s, M-T Co., 19" long, minor toy, includes two tin cars
    $300.00 $600.00   7

Space Trip Station, 1960s, Yonezawa Co., 13½" long, four actions, includes four plastic satellites
    $700.00 $1,400.00+   10

Spaceman Robot, 1950s, Linemar, 7½" tall, three actions
    $500.00 $1,000.00+   8

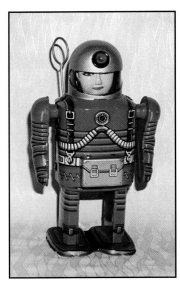

Spaceman Robot, 1950s, T-N Co., 9¼" tall, three actions
    $500.00 $1,000.00   8

Spaceman With Light On Head, 1956, Daiya Co., Linemar, 7" tall, three actions
    $600.00 $1,200.00   9

Spanking Bear, 1950s, Linemar Co., 9" high, six actions
    $150.00 $300.00   4

Sparking Burp Gun, 1950s, Marx Co., 24" long, three actions
    $40.00 $80.00   2

Sparkling Mike the Robot, 1950s, Ace Co., 7½" tall, three actions
    $1,000.00 $2,000.00+   10

Sparky Savings Bank, 1930s, Byron Co., 4" long, 4½" high doghouse, electro-magnet action, includes 4" long compo dog, minor toy
    $60.00 $120.00   4

Sparky the Seal, 1950s, M-T Co., 6" high, 7" long, four actions, two cycles, includes celluloid ball
    $80.00 $160.00   2

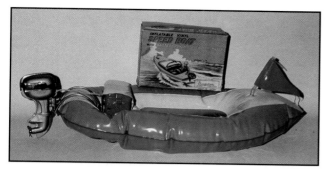

Speed Boat with Battery Powered Outboard Motor and Inflatable Vinyl Boat, 1950s, Cragstan Co., 15" long, minor toy
$100.00 $200.00   7

Speedboat G-3, 1950s, I.T.O. Co., 13" long, minor toy
$130.00 $260.00   7

Speed Control Racer With 5 Gear Shift, 1960s, Daiya Co., 9" long, four actions
$200.00 $400.00   6

Speed Jack—Mongoose Hot Rod, 1950s, Taiyo Co., 10¼" long, three actions
$100.00 $200.00   5

Speed King Racer, 1960s, Y Co., 12½" long, three actions
$70.00 $140.00   5

Speed King-U-Control Racing Car, 1960s, S & E Co., 9½" long, three actions, marked #7
$150.00 $300.00   6

Speed Racer With Blinking Signal Lights, 1950s, T-N Co., 11" long, four actions, marked #25
$160.00 $320.00   6

Spin-A-Disk Monkey, 1950s, S&E Co., 10" tall, six actions, includes tin hat and disc
$150.00 $300.00   6

Spirit of 1776, Locomotive No. 4406, 1976 M-T Co., 15¾" long, five actions
$40.00 $80.00   2

Sports Car Race Set, 1960s, TPS Co., 8"x14" base, minor toy, includes four plastic racecars
$100.00 $200.00   2

Squirrel, see Animated Squirrel

Star Strider, Robot, 1980s, S-H Co., 12" tall, six actions
$110.00 $220.00   1

Stagecoach, 1950s, Daiya Co., 13" long, four actions
$110.00 $220.00   6

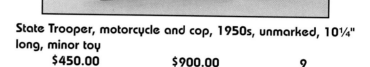

State Trooper, motorcycle and cop, 1950s, unmarked, 10¼" long, minor toy
$450.00 $900.00   9

Steam Roller, 1950s, Y Co., 8" long, four actions, includes tin trailer
$100.00 $200.00   4

Steam Roller, Road Roller, 1950s, T-N Co., Rosko, 12" long with trailer, four actions
$90.00 $180.00   4

Steerable Tank, 1950s, Linemar Co., 9" long, five actions
$60.00 $120.00   4

Stick Shifters—Blue Slick Racer, 1972, Hasbro Co., 10½" long, minor toy, includes 9" plastic racer
$30.00 $60.00   3

Stop—Go Coin Driver Bank, 1950s, Marusan Col., 9½" long, three actions, truck
$170.00 $340.00   6

Strange Explorer, 1960s, DSK Co., 7½" long, four actions
$125.00 $250.00   2

Strato Jet U.S.A.F., 1950s, T-N Co., 13" long, 14" wingspan, three actions
     $120.00 $240.00   5

Streamliner, 1950s, Cragstan Co., 18" long assembled, minor toy, includes truck and remote control
     $60.00 $120.00   6

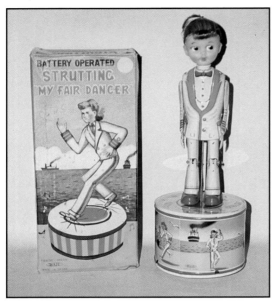

Strutting My Fair Dancer, Dancing Sailor Girl, 1950s, Haji Co., 12" tall, two pieces, minor toy
     $100.00 $200.00   **3**

Strutting Sam, 1950s, Haji Co., 10½" tall, minor jigger toy
     $200.00 $400.00   4

Stunt Car, 1960s, M-T Co., 10½" long, minor toy
     $50.00 $100.00   3

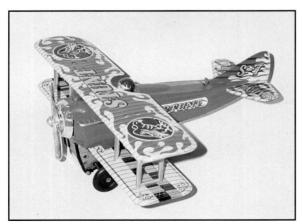

Stunt Plane–Spad III, 1960s, TPS Co., 9" long, 10½" wingspan, three actions
     $100.00 $200.00   5

Sunbeam Jeep No. 1, 1940s, 10", Marusan Co., three actions
     $100.00 $200.00   5

Sunbeam Side Car, 1950s, Marusan Co., 9½" long, three actions, motorcycle
     $700.00 $1,400.00   9

Sunday Driver, 1950s, M-T Co., 10" long, four actions, includes detachable driver
     $70.00 $140.00   2

Super Astronaut Robot, 1960s, S-H Co., 11½" tall, five actions, two cycles
     $110.00 $220.00   1

Super Astronaut Robot, 1960s, SJM Co., 12" tall, four actions
     $150.00 $300.00   2

Super Blender, 1960s, Alps Co., 9¾" high, minor toy, mostly plastic
     $20.00 $40.00   2

Super Command Rifle, 1950s, S-H Co., 16" long, minor toy
     $40.00 $80.00   2

Super Flying Police Helicopter, 1960s, TPS Co., 11½" long, six actions, includes detachable plastic rotor

$90.00 $180.00   6

Super Giant Robot, 1960s, S-H Co., 15½" tall, six actions

$200.00 $400.00   4

Super Greyhound Bus, 1950s, Stone Co., 11" long, four actions

$70.00 $140.00   3

Super Jet, 1950s, T-N Co., 12" long, 8" wingspan, three actions

$250.00 $500.00   6

Super News Copter, 1960s, S-H Co., 16" long, six actions, includes detachable tin rotor

$100.00 $200.00   5

Super Sonic Space Rocket, 1950s, K-O Co., 14" l, four actions

$240.00 $480.00   8

Super Space Capsule, 1960s, S-H Co., 9" high, four actions

$100.00 $200.00   3

Super Space Commander, 1960s, S-H Co., 10" tall, four actions, mostly plastic, a.k.a. Ranger Robot

$70.00 $140.00   3

Super Susie, 1950s, Linemar Co., 9" high, six actions

$400.00 $800.00   6

Superior Ambulance, 1960s, Asakusa Toy Co., 11¾" long, three actions

$150.00 $300.00   8

Surrey Jeep, 1960s, T-N Co., 11" long, three actions
$90.00 $180.00   5

Suzy-Q Automatic Ironer, 1950s, GW Co., 7" high, four actions

$90.00 $180.00   5

Suzette the Eating Monkey, 1950s, Linemar Co., 8¾" high, 7"x5" base, five actions, includes tin litho steak
$300.00 $600.00   7

Swan—The Queen On The River, 1960s, Meiho Co., 8½" high, 7½" long, four actions
$60.00 $120.00   8

Superman Tank, 1950s, Linemar Co., 10¼" long, three actions

$600.00 $1,200.00+   9

Swimming Duck, 1950s, Bandai Co., 8" long, four actions
$90.00 $180.00   8

Swing Tail Cargo Plane—Flying Tiger, 1960s, T-N Co., 14" long, 14" wingspan, five actions
$300.00 $600.00   5

Switchboard Operator, 1950s, Linemar, 7½" high, four actions

$350.00	**$700.00**	**6**

Swivel-O-Matic Astronaut, robot, 1960s, S-H Co., 11½" tall, five actions, two cycles

$80.00	$160.00	1

T 360 Monoplane, see Bristol Bulldog Airplane

T.V. Broadcasting Van, 1960s, VW, Gakken Co., 7½" long, three actions, includes detachable antenna

$100.00	$200.00	5

Talking Dalek, 1975, Politoy Co., 7" tall, minor toy

$150.00	$300.00	6

Talking Dalek–BBC, 1975, Hong Kong, 7" high, minor toy, mostly plastic, British T.V. character

$70.00	$140.00	2

Talking Police Car–Mystery Action, 1960s, Y Co., 14" long, three actions

$70.00	$140.00	2

Talking Robot, 1960s, Yonezawa Co., 10¾" tall, three actions

$600.00	$1,200.00	9

Talking Trixie, 1950s, Alps Co., 6½" long, four actions

$40.00	$80.00	6

Tank M-4 Combat Tank, 1960s, Taiyo Co., 11½" long, 13" with gun barrel extended, five actions

$80.00	$160.00	3

Tank M-35, 1950s, HTC Co., 8" long, three actions

$100.00	$200.00	3

Tank M-41, 1970s, J Co., 8¼" long, four actions

$100.00	$200.00	3

Tank M-48T, 1960s, T-N Co., 8¼" long, four actions

$90.00	$180.00	2

Tank M-56, 1940s, M-T Co., 7½" long, wheel drive, seven actions

$100.00	$200.00	3

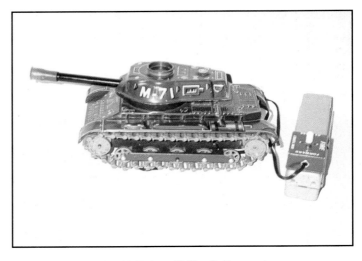

Tank M-71, 1950s, M-T Co., 8¾" tall, five actions

$90.00	**$180.00**	**3**

Tank M-81, 1960s, M-T Co., 8½" long, seven actions

$100.00	$200.00	3

Tank M-103, 1950s, M-T Co., 7" long, three actions

$90.00	$180.00	3

Tank M-107–US Army, 1950s, Y Co., 6" long, four actions, includes four missiles

$120.00	$240.00	4

Tank M-X, 1950s, T-N Co., 8½" long, five actions

$70.00	$140.00	3

Tank T-5, 1950s, T-N Co., 8½" long, three actions, includes detachable radar antenna

$110.00	$220.00	3

Tank 392–U.S. Tank Division, 1950s, Marx Co., 9½" long, three actions

$70.00	$140.00	3

Tank X-3, (explorer defense), 1950s, Cragstan Co., 7¾" long, five actions, includes six cartridge shells
$130.00 $260.00   4

Tank X-75, 1950s, M-T Co., 9" long, three actions, includes tin gun and darts
$110.00 $220.00   4

Tank–Daisymatic No. 64 Rapid Fire Tank, 1960s, Daisy Mfg. Co., 8" long, four actions
$120.00 $240.00   5

Tank–Daisymatic No. 80, 1965, Daisy Mfg. Co., 8½" long, five actions, includes darts
$100.00 $200.00   5

Tank Robot, 1960s, S-H Co., 10" tall, five actions
$300.00 $600.00   7

Tarzan, 1966, Marusan Co., (Banner), 13" tall, four actions
$500.00 $1,000.00+   9

Taxes–Taxes–Bank, 1960s, unmarked, 9" long, minor toy, mostly plastic
$90.00 $180.00   7

Taxi, (yellow cab), 1950s, Linemar Co., 7½" long, five actions
$100.00 $200.00   5

Taxi Cab, 1960s, Y Co., 9" long, four actions
$90.00 $180.00   4

Teddy–Balloon Blowing Bear, 1950s, Alps Co., 11½" high, six actions
$90.00 $180.00   2

Teddy Bear Circus Acrobat, 1950s, Tomiyana Co., 15" high, three actions, includes detachable bear flyer
$500.00 $1,000.00   8

Teddy Bear Swing, 1950s, T-N Co., 17" high, three actions, two cycles, includes four wire supports and tin sign
$250.00 $500.00   7

Teddy-Go-Kart, 1960s, Alps Co., 10½" long, four actions
$100.00 $200.00   5

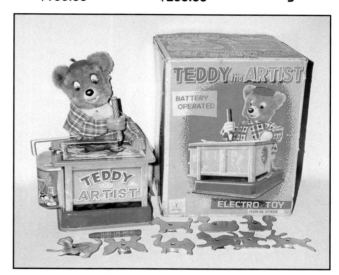

Teddy the Artist, 1950s, Y Co., 8½" high, 5¼"x7" base, three actions, includes removable tray and nine patterns
$300.00 $600.00   5

Teddy the Champ Boxer, 1950s, Y Co., 9" tall, five actions
$150.00 $300.00   4

Teddy the Manager, 1950s, S&E Co., 8" high, six actions
$300.00 $600.00   6

Teddy the Rhythmical Drummer, 1960s, Alps Co., 11" tall, three actions
$100.00 $200.00   4

Telephone Bear, 1950s, Linemar, 7½" high, six actions
$160.00 $320.00   5

Telephone Bear–Ringing And Talking In <u>Her</u> Old Rocking Chair, 1950s, M-T Co., 10" high, four actions
$150.00 $300.00   6

Telephone Bear–Ringing and Talking in <u>His</u> Old Rocking Chair, 1950s, M-T Co., 10" high, four actions

$150.00 $300.00   6

Telephone Bear–Winky Eyes, 1950s, T-N Co., 8" high, six actions

$150.00 $300.00   6

Telephone Bear–With Lights, 1950s, Linemar Co., 8" high, six actions

$140.00 $280.00   6

Telephone Rabbit–Ringing And Talking In <u>Her</u> Old Rocking Chair, 1950s, M-T Co., 10" high, four actions

$150.00 $300.00   7

Telephone Rabbit Ringing And Talking In <u>His</u> Old Rocking Chair, 1950s, M-T Co., 10" high, four actions

$170.00 $340.00   6

Telephone Talking Bear, 1950s, M-T Co., 9" high, four actions

$150.00 $300.00   8

Television Truck With Movable Cameramen And Cameras, 1950s, a.k.a. NAR Television Truck, Linemar Co., 11" long, five actions, includes six strip films

$300.00 $600.00   7

Television Spaceman, 1960s, Alps Co., 14½" high to tip of antenna, six actions

$400.00 $800.00   7

Tempo VI Speed Boat, 1950s, M-T Co., 9¾" long, three actions

$90.00 $180.00   7

Terry The Wonder Dog With Lighted Eyes, 1960s, Linemar Co., 8" long, 9" high, three actions

$40.00 $80.00   4

Texaco Toy Tanker, (North Dakota), 1960s, A.M.F. Co., minor toy, includes detachable masts and figures

$60.00 $120.00   2

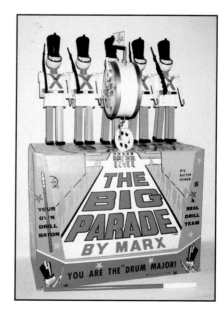

The Big Parade, 1963, Marx Co., 11½" tall, 15" wide, four actions, includes detachable guns and baton

$120.00 $240.00   2

The Chimp And Pup Rail Car, 1950s, Cragstan Co., 9" long, four actions
$110.00 $220.00   8

The Dolphin, (with Evenrude Outboard Motor), 1960s, Fleet Line Co., 12" long, minor toy, mostly plastic
$130.00 $260.00   5

The Fiesta Queen, (with inboard motor), 1950s, Fleet Line Co., 11" long, minor toy, mostly wood
$70.00 $140.00   4

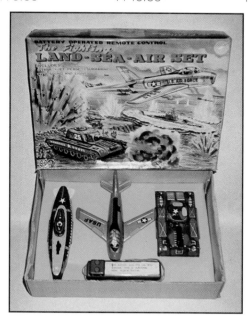

The Fighting-Land-Sea-Air Set, 1950s, Marx Co., four piece set-tank, 5" long, submarine 8" long, jet airplane 7" long, three actions
$200.00   **$400.00**   **8**

The Jolly Peanut Vendor, 1950s, T-N Co., 8" high, five actions, includes detachable felt hat
$210.00   **$420.00**   **4**

The Laughing Clown, 1960s, S-H Co., 15" tall, six actions
$210.00 $420.00   5

The Laughing Robot, 1960s, S-H Co., 13½" tall, six actions
$150.00 $300.00   3

The Loser, (Bar Toy), 1971, Poynter Prod. Co., 13" high, three actions
$40.00   **$80.00**   **1**

The Marlin, (with Scott-Atwater Outboard Motor), 1960s, Fleet Line Co., 12" long, minor toy, mostly plastic
$140.00 $280.00   6

The Marx-Tronic Electric Train System, (The Train With A Brain), 1950s, Marx Co., 16" long assembled, seven actions, includes 12 ft. of plastic track
$60.00 $120.00   6

The Pink Panther, 1970s, ILLCO Co., Taiwan, 11" high, six actions, includes detachable drums and cymbals
$60.00   **$120.00**   **3**

The Playing Monkey, 1950s, S&E Co., (Ahi Brand), 10" tall, six actions, includes detachable hat and tin yo-yo
$200.00 $400.00   6

The Rabbits and Carriage, 1950s, S&E Co., 10" tall, 1950s, M-T Co., four actions, should have tin butterfly

$150.00 $300.00   4

The Sea Babe, (with inboard motor), 1950s, Fleet Line Co., 18" long, minor toy, mostly wood

$100.00 $200.00   6

The Sea Comber, (with outboard motor), 1960s, Fleet Line Co., 18½" long with motor, minor toy, mostly plastic

$100.00 $200.00   6

The Sea Wolf, (with inboard motor), 1950s, Fleet Line Co., 18" long, minor toy, mostly wood

$70.00 $140.00   4

The Swinger—Mustang Mach 1, 1960s, T.P.S. Co., 10½" long, three actions

$60.00 $120.00   1

The Thing—From The Addams Family, 1964, Poynter Prod. Co., 4½" long, minor toy

$40.00   **$80.00**   1

The Viking, (with Johnson Outboard Motor), 1960s, Fleet Line Co., 11" long, mostly plastic

$110.00   **$220.00**   **6**

Thunder Jet, 1950s, Bandai Co., 9¾" long, three actions

$130.00 $260.00   5

Thunder Robot, 1950s, Asakusa Co., 11½" tall, six actions

$1,500.00 $3,000.00+   9

Thunderbird Speedster With Automatic Action, 1950s, T-N Co., 11" long, five actions

310.00 $620.00   7

Thundermatic Tank—Daisymatic #64, 1950s, Daisy Mfg. Co., 8½" long, three actions, includes detachable gun barrel, mostly plastic

$60.00 $120.00   5

Tin Man, Robot, 1960s, Remco Industries, Inc., 21" tall, all plastic, four actions, mostly plastic

$100.00 $200.00   3

Tinkling Locomotive, 1960s, M-T Co., 9½" long, four actions

$40.00 $80.00   5

Tinkling Trolley, 1950s, M-T Co., 10½" long, four actions, two cycles, includes two plastic cowcatchers, two variations

$110.00   **$220.00**   **2**

Tiny Jeep, 1950s, WACO Co., 4¼" long, minor action

$30.00 $60.00   4

Tiny Tank, 1950s, WACO Co., 4¼" long, minor action

$30.00 $60.00   4

Tippy Tumbles, 1968, Remco Co., 16" tall, minor toy

$30.00 $60.00   3

Tom and Jerry Auto, 1960s, Rico Co., (Spain), 13" long, three actions

$400.00 $800.00   9

Tom and Jerry Choo Choo, 1960s, M-T Co., 10¼" long, five actions

$120.00 $240.00   4

Tom and Jerry Comic Car, 1960s, M-T Co., 11" long, three actions

$150.00 $300.00   5

Tom and Jerry Formula Racing Car, 1960s, M-T Co., 11" long, three actions
$90.00 $180.00   3

Tom and Jerry Hand Car–Jerry, 1960s, M-T Co., 9¾" high, 7¾" long, three actions
$130.00 $260.00   3

Tom and Jerry Hand Car–Tom, 1960s, M-T Co., 9¾" high, 7¾" long, three actions
$130.00 $260.00   3

Tom and Jerry Helicopter, 1960s, M-T Co., 9½" long, three actions
$110.00 $220.00   3

Tom and Jerry Highway Patrol, 1960s, M-T Co., 8" long, three actions
$120.00 $240.00   4

Tom and Jerry Jumping Jeep, 1960s, M-T Co., 9" long, three actions
$120.00 $240.00   4

Tom and Jerry Locomotive, 1960s, M-T Co., 9" long, six actions, (Jerry)
$80.00 $160.00   5

Tom and Jerry Locomotive, 1960s, M-T Co., 9" long, six actions (Tom)
$80.00 $160.00   4

Tom Tom Indian, 1960s, Y Co., 10½" tall, four actions
$80.00 $160.00   4

Tootin' Tin Lizzie, (?), 1950s, Alps Co., 7" long, minor toy
$40.00 $80.00   5

Topo Gigio Xylophone Player, 1960s, T-N Co., 10½" high, three actions, includes detachable xylophone
$500.00 $1,000.00+   10

Torpedo Boat–PT 107, 1950s, Linemar 11½" long, three actions
$110.00 $220.00   5

Tractor, 1950s, Showa Co., 7½" long, four actions, includes litho tin figure, (driver)
$60.00 $120.00   2

Tractor, 1960s, Y Co., 6" long, three actions
$50.00 $100.00   2

Tractor On Platform, 1950s, T-N Co., tractor 9" long, trailer 7" long, minor toy
$80.00 $160.00   3

Tractor With Visible Lighted Piston Movement, 1950s, Linemar Co., 10" long, four actions, includes detachable tin driver
$150.00 $300.00   5

Traffic Policeman, 1950s, A-I Co., 14" tall, 6"x6" base, four actions
$250.00 $500.00   6

Trans American Express, 1950s, Y Co., 18" long assembled, three actions, includes locomotive, three cars, and five sections of track
$50.00 $100.00   5

Tubby the Turtle, 1950s, Y Co., 7" long, three actions
$50.00　　　　**$100.00**　　　　**4**

Traveler Bear, 1950s, K Co., 8" tall, three actions
$180.00　　　　**$360.00**　　　　**7**

Treasure Chest, Bank, 1960s, Illfelder Co., 11" tall, five actions, two cycles, risque toy, PG rated
$90.00　　　　$180.00　　　　1

Tric–cycling Clown, 1960s, M-T Co., 12" high, five actions
$300.00　　　　$600.00　　　　8

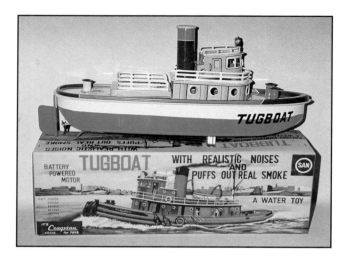

Tugboat, 1950s, Marusan Co., 13½" long, three actions
$110.00　　　　**$220.00**　　　　**2**

Tricky Dog House, No. 673, 1960s, Y Co., 6¾" high, 7¼" long, 6¾" wide, four actions
$60.00　　　　**$120.00**　　　　**2**

Tugboat Neptune, 1950s, M-T Co., 14½" long, five actions
$100.00　　　　$200.00　　　　3

Tugboat With Shaking Action And Sound, 1950s, Marx Co., 6½" long, three actions
$90.00　　　　$180.00　　　　8

Tricky Tommy–the Big Brain Tractor, 1950s, Marx Co., 10" long, three actions
$100.00　　　　$200.00　　　　4

Tulip Head Robot, see Space Robot with T.V. Camera and Screen

Triumph Coupe, 1950s, Bandai Co., 8" long, four actions
$60.00　　　　$120.00　　　　6

Tumbles the Bear, 1960s, Y-M Co., Yanoman, 8½" tall, minor toy, includes porter's hat
$80.00　　　　$160.00　　　　2

Trumpet Playing Bunny, 1950s, Alps Co., 10" high, four actions, includes tin horn
$150.00　　　　$300.00　　　　5

Tumbling Bozo The Clown, 1970s, Sonsco Co., Hong Kong, 1971, 8" long, minor toy
$75.00　　　　$150.00　　　　6

Turn Signal Robot, 1960s, T-N Co., 11" tall, five actions, Auto Accessory, a.k.a. Monsturn
$160.00　　　　$320.00　　　　2

Trumpet Playing Monkey, 1950s, Alps Co., 9" high, four actions, includes tin horn
$170.00　　　　$340.00　　　　4

Turn-O-Matic Gun Jeep, 1960s, T-N Co., 10" long, five actions
$100.00　　　　$200.00　　　　4

Turn-O-Matic Gun Patrol Car, 1960s, T-N Co., 10" long, five actions

$110.00	$220.00	5

Turntable Xylophone Melody Train, 1960s, Cragstan Co., 29½" long assembled, three actions

$50.00	$100.00	3

TWA DC-9 Airliner, 1960s, T-M Co., 16" long, 14" wingspan, six actions

$140.00	$280.00	6

TWA Multiaction DC-7C Airliner, 1960s, Yonezawa Coi., 22½" long, 23¼" wingspan, seven actions

$200.00	$400.00	6

Tweety Bird Lantern, lantern toy, 1950s, Amico Co., 5½" high

$40.00	**$80.00**	**7**

Twin Coupled Tram Cars, 1950s, K Co., minor toy, 11½" long, two cars

$100.00	$200.00	6

Twin Racing Cars, 1950s, Alps Co., 7" long, 10" long with coupling rod, three actions

$300.00	**$600.00**	**6**

Twinkle Twinkle Christmas Lantern, lantern toy, 1950s, Amico Co., 5" high, minor toy, includes interchangeable Christmas tree

$100.00	$200.00	9

Twirly Whirly, 1950s, Alps Co., 13½" high, four actions, same as Coney Island Rocket Ride

$400.00	$800.00	6

Twist Dancer, (Let's Twist), 1960s, no mfr. mark, 15" high, minor toy, a.k.a. The Twister

$100.00	$200.00	5

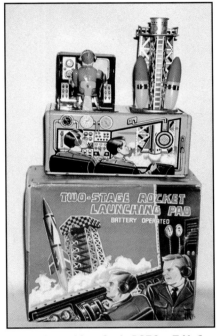

Two-Stage Rocket Launching Pad, 1950s, T-N Co., 7" long, 4" wide, 8" high, three actions, includes two plastic-rubber rockets

$250.00	**$500.00**	**6**

Tyrannosaurus, 1970s, Toytown Co., 9" long, four actions, mostly plastic

$80.00	$160.00	3

UFO–X05, 1970s, M-T Co., 7½" diameter, three actions

$50.00	$100.00	1

Union Mountain Cable Lines, Monorail Set, 1950s, T-N Co., car 8" long, 16 piece oval track, 22"x32", minor toy

$80.00	$160.00	2

United DC7 Mainliner, 1950s, Yonezaqa Co., 19" long, 14" wingspan, five actions

$200.00	$400.00	6

United Mainliner Stratocruiser, 1950s, Linemar, 19½" long, 13" wingspan, four actions

$190.00	$380.00	5

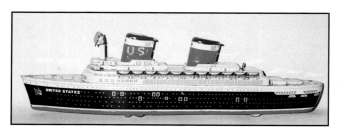

United States Ocean Liner, 1950s, Linemar Co., 14" long, three actions

$200.00	$400.00	5

United States Ocean Liner, 1950s, Y Co., 18½" long, three actions

$300.00	$600.00	5

Universal Machine Gun, 1950s, T-N Co., 14¾" long, three actions

$70.00	$140.00	3

Universal Traveler, 1950s, Bandai Co., 9½" long, 9" wingspan, 4" diameter, tin globe, minor toy

$180.00	$360.00	9

USA—NASA Apollo Space Ship, 1960s, M-T Co., 9" long, four actions

$150.00	$300.00	4

USA—NASA Gemini Space Capsule, 1960s, M-T Co., 9" long, four actions, includes detachable astronaut

$120.00	$240.00	5

U.S.A.F. Gemini X-5, 1960s, M-T Co., 9" long, four actions, vehicle includes detachable plastic antenna

$90.00	$180.00	4

U.S. Air Force Military Airlift Command Jet, 1960s, T-N Co., 14" wingspan, four actions

$130.00	$260.00	5

U.S. Navy Pom Pom Gun, 1950s, Remco Co., 20" long, four actions

$80.00	$160.00	4

U.S. Royal Tire—Mechanical Toy, (Ferris Wheel) souvenir for 1964-65 N.Y. World's Fair (now permanently located at Uniroyal Co., on Rt. 94, west of Detroit), 10" high, includes plastic figures, minor toy, Ideal

$100.00	$200.00	3

U.S.S. Battlewagon—400, 1963, Deluxe Reading Corp., 33" long, four actions, mostly plastic, includes plastic jets, torpedoes, and ammunition

$110.00	$220.00	8

U-Turn Cadillac, 1950s, K-O Co., 8¾" long, five actions

$70.00	$140.00	8

V-8 Roadster, (#8), 1960s, Daiya Co., 11" long, four actions

$140.00	$280.00	7

Venus Robot, 1960s, K-O Co., 5½" tall, minor toy

$100.00	$200.00	5

Vertibird, 1971, Mattel Co., 24" long, minor toy, includes rescue spot, raft, space capsule and astronaut

$100.00	$200.00	5

Vertical Liner, 1960s, Robert Simpson, Ltd., for Sears, 18½" long, five actions

$250.00	$500.00	7

Veteran Car, 1950s, Z Co., 9½" long, four actions

$110.00	$220.00	8

Video Robot, 1960s, S-H Co., 10" tall, three actions

$90.00	$180.00	3

V.I.P. the Busy Boss, 1950s, S&E Co., 8" high, six actions

$220.00	$440.00	3

Visible Ford Mustang, 1960s, Bandai Co., 10" long, four actions

$80.00	$160.00	3

Vision Robot, 1960s, S-H Co., 11¾" tall, five actions
$150.00 $300.00   4

Voice Control Astronaut Base, 1969, Remco Co., 19" long, four actions, includes plastic missiles and phonograph records
$90.00 $180.00   4

Volkswagen Convertible, 1950s, T-N Co., 9¾" long, three actions
$250.00 $500.00   6

Volkswagen, 1960s, Taiyo Co., 10" long, three actions
$60.00 $120.00   3

Volkswagen–Elektrik, 1950s, Mignon Co., 8½" long, three actions
$70.00 $140.00   5

Volkswagen No. 7653, 1960s, Bandai Co., 10" long, three actions
$90.00 $180.00   4

Volkswagen with Visible Engine, 1960s, K.O. Co., 7" long, three actions
$80.00 $160.00   3

Volkswagen with Visible Engine No. 4049, 1960s, Bandai Co., 8" long, three actions
$90.00 $180.00   3

Waddles Family Car, 1960s, Y Co., 6" long, minor toy
$40.00 $80.00   4

Wagon Master, 1960s, M-T Co., 18" long, four actions
$120.00 $240.00   5

Walking And Climbing Fireman, 1950s, Sonsco Co., 24" long, extended ladder and 7" tall fireman, three actions
$140.00 $280.00   7

Walking Bambi, 1950s, Linemar Co., 9" high, 8½" long, four actions
$200.00 $400.00   9

Walking Bear with Xylophone, 1950s, Linemar Co., 10" high, seven actions
$300.00 $600.00   9

Walking Cat, 1950s, Linemar Co., 6" long, three actions
$40.00 $80.00   4

Walking Dog, 1950s, Linemar Co., 6" long, five actions
$60.00 $120.00   6

Walking Donkey, 1950s, Linemar Co., 9" high, three actions
$90.00 $180.00   6

Walking Elephant, 1950s, Linemar Co., 8½" long, three actions
$90.00 $180.00   5

Walking Gorilla, 1950s, Linemar Co., 7½" tall, three actions
$150.00 $300.00   5

Walking Itchy Dog, 1950s, Alps Co., 9" long, five actions
$60.00 $120.00   3

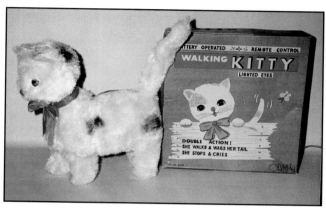

Walking Kitty, 1950s, Olympia Co., 8½" tall, five actions, two cycles
$90.00   **$180.00**   **3**

Walking Knight In Armor, 1950s, M-T Co., 11" tall, five actions, remote control
$1,000.00 $2,000.00+   10

Walking Musical Series—Cellist, 1970s, T-N Co., 8¾" high, three actions, mostly plastic
$50.00 $100.00   7

Walking Musical Series—Drummer, 1970s, T-N Co., 5¼" high, three actions, mostly plastic
$50.00   **$100.00**   **7**

Walking Robot, 1950s, Y Co., 6" tall, minor toy, also made with a dome on head
$500.00 $1,000.00+   9

Walking Tiger, 1950s, Marx Co., 11½" tall, four actions, a.k.a. Esso Tiger

    $250.00   **$500.00**   **6**

Walky-Son (Los), see Los Walky Son

Walt Disney's Tomorrowland-Moon Orbit, 1960, Wen-Mac Co., 20" high assembled, minor toy, 15 piece set

    $200.00 $400.00   9

Walt Disney's Tomorrowland-Rocket Ride, 1960, Wen-Mac Co., 29" high assembled, minor toy, 38 piece set

    $200.00 $400.00   9

Walt Disney's Tomorrowland-Space Wheel, 1960, Wen-Mac Co., 28" high assembled, minor toy, 27 piece set

    $200.00 $400.00   9

Warpath Indian, 1950s, Alps Co., 12" tall, three actions

    $80.00 $160.00   5

Wash-O-Matic, washing machine, 1940s, T-N Co., 5¾" high, 4¼" diameter, minor toy, includes lid

    $30.00 $60.00   3

Water Spouting Whale with Flopping Tail, 1950s, KKS Co., 13" long, minor toy

    $100.00 $200.00   5

Wee Little Baby Bear, 1950s, Alps Co., 9" high, four actions, a.k.a. Reading Bear

    $160.00 $320.00   9

Western Badman, (Red Gulch Bar), 1960s, M-T Co., 9¾" high, eight actions, includes three plastic bottles, and two plastic glasses

    $300.00   **$600.00**   **7**

Western Express Locomotive, 1960s, Kanto Toy Co., 14" long, four actions

    $50.00 $100.00   1

Western Flyer—Big Switcher Train Set, 1950s, Y Co., 15½" long assembled, thirteen piece set, minor toy

    $60.00   **$120.00**   **8**

Western Locomotive, 1950s, M-T Co., 10½" long, four actions

    $50.00 $100.00   1

Western Style Music Box, 1950s, 5" high, minor toy

    $100.00 $200.00   7

Wheel-A-Gear, Robot, 1960s, Taiyo Co., 14½" tall, five actions

    $400.00 $800.00   8

WHOH—Skyway Patrol Helicopter, 1950s, M-T Co., 18" long, four actions

    $100.00 $200.00   7

Whirlybird Helicopter, 1960s, Remco Co., 25" long, three actions

$80.00 $160.00   4

Whistling Showboat, 1950s, M-T Co., 14" long, three actions

$120.00 $240.00   3

Whistling Spooky Kooky Tree, 1950s, Marx Co., 14¼" tall, six actions, two variations

$500.00   **$1,000.00+**   **5**

Wild West Rodeo, see Bubbling Bull

Willy The Walking Car, 1960s, Y Co., 8½" long, six actions

$110.00 $220.00   7

Windsor Talking Slot Machine, Yonezawa Co., 1960s, 10½" high, minor toy

$60.00 $120.00   4

Windy the Elephant, 1950s, T-N Co., 9¾" high, three actions, includes celluloid ball and tin litho umbrella

$140.00 $280.00   4

Winking Merry Lite, lantern toy, 1950s, M-S Co., 6" high, minor toy

$20.00 $40.00   3

Winner—23, Rocket, 1950s, KDP Co., Excelo, 5½" long, minor actions, includes rubber track

$150.00 $300.00   6

Winner of the West, Overland Stagecoach with Four Galloping Horses, 1950s, Alps Co., 18" long, four actions

$200.00 $400.00   7

Winston the Barking Bulldog, 1950s, Tomiyama Co., 10" long, three actions, two cycles

$70.00 $140.00   4

Wonder Loco, 1970s, Taiyo Kogyo Co., 8" long, four actions

$10.00 $20.00   1

Wonderland Locomotive, 1960s, Bandai Co., 9" long, three actions

$40.00 $80.00   3

Wood Model Boat #70065, 1950s, M-H–M Co., 10½" long, minor toy, mostly wood

$60.00 $120.00   4

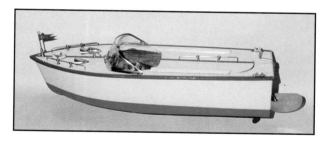

Wood Model Motor-Boat #70065, 1950s, S-W Co., 11" long, minor toy, mostly wood

$60.00   **$120.00**   **5**

World Champion, 1950s, M-T Co., 11" long, five actions, motorcycle with Howdy Doody look-alike driver

$700.00 $1,4000+   10

World Globe, lantern toy, 1950s, Amico Co., 6" high, minor toy

$50.00 $100.00   6

XM-12 Moon Rocket, 1950s, Y Co., 15" long, three actions

$210.00	$420.00	8

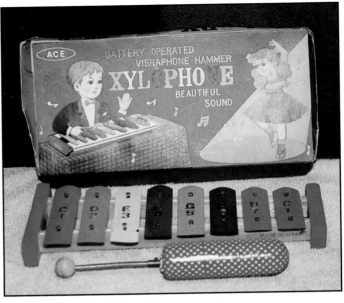

Xylophone, 1950s, Ace Co., 6" long, minor toy

$20.00	$40.00	7

Yellow Cab, see Taxi

Yellow Cab Bank, see Coin Operated Battery Cab

Worried Mother Duck and Baby, 1950s, T-N Co., 11" long, 7" high, three actions

$100.00	$200.00	4

X-7 Space Explorer Ship, 1960s, M-T Co., 7" diameter, four actions

$90.00	$180.00	4

X-9 Space Robot Car, 1950'sa M-T Co., 9½" long, five actions

$1,500.00	$3,000.00+	10

X-07 Surveillant, 1960s, T-N Co., 9½" long, three actions

$200.00	$400.00	7

X-16 Space Patrol, see Space Patrol With Floating Satellite

X-70 Robot, see Space Robot With T. V. Camera And Screen

X-80 Planet Explorer, 1960s, M-T Co., 8" diameter, four actions

$90.00	$180.00	6

X-1800 Space Vehicle, 1960s, M-T Co., 9" long, five actions, includes detachable plastic antenna

$140.00	$280.00	6

X-F 160 Jet Airplane, 1960s, K-O Co., 8" wingspan, four actions

$80.00	$160.00	5

Yeti the Abominable Snowman, 1960s, Marx Co., 12" tall, four actions

$300.00	$600.00	6

Yo-Yo Clown, 1960s, Alps Co., 9" high, three actions, includes plastic yo-yo

$170.00	$340.00	7

Zoom Boat, 1950s, K Co., 12" long, three actions
$90.00 $180.00   4

Yo-Yo Clown, 1960s, S&E Co., 10" tall, five actions, includes plastic yo-yo
$150.00 $300.00   7

Yo-Yo Monkey, 1960s, Alps Co., 9" tall, three actions, includes plastic yo-yo
$140.00 $280.00   5

Yo-Yo Monkey, 1960s, Y-M Co., 12" tall, spring extension to 32", minor
$100.00 $200.00   5

Yummy-Yum Kitten—With Fish, 1950s, Linemar Co., 9" tall, five actions
$250.00 $500.00   9

Zero Fighter Plane, 1950s, Bandai Co., 12½" long, 15" wingspan, three actions
$160.00 $320.00   3

Zero-Zip Gun, 1970s, Tomy Co., 8" long, minor toy, lanyard
$20.00 $40.00   4

Zoomer the Robot, 1950s, T-N Co., 8" tall, three actions
$250.00 $500.00   5

COLLECTOR BOOKS

I n f o r m i n g   T o d a y ' s   C o l l e c t o r

For over two decades we have been keeping collectors informed on trends and values in all fields of antiques and collectibles.

DOLLS, FIGURES & TEDDY BEARS

4707	A Decade of **Barbie** Dolls & Collectibles, 1981–1991, Summers	$19.95
4631	**Barbie** Doll Boom, 1986–1995, Augustyniak	$18.95
2079	**Barbie** Doll Fashions, Volume I, Eames	$24.95
3957	**Barbie** Exclusives, Rana	$18.95
4632	**Barbie** Exclusives, Book II, Rana	$18.95
4557	**Barbie**, The First 30 Years, Deutsch	$24.95
4657	**Barbie** Years, 1959–1995, Olds	$16.95
3310	**Black Dolls**, 1820–1991, Perkins	$17.95
3873	**Black Dolls**, Book II, Perkins	$17.95
1529	Collector's Encyclopedia of **Barbie** Dolls, DeWein	$19.95
4506	Collector's Guide to **Dolls in Uniform**, Bourgeois	$18.95
3727	Collector's Guide to **Ideal Dolls**, Izen	$18.95
3728	Collector's Guide to Miniature **Teddy Bears**, Powell	$17.95
3967	Collector's Guide to **Trolls**, Peterson	$19.95
4571	**Liddle Kiddles**, Identification & Value Guide, Langford	$18.95
4645	**Madame Alexander** Dolls Price Guide #21, Smith	$9.95
3733	**Modern Collector's** Dolls, Sixth Series, Smith	$24.95
3991	**Modern Collector's** Dolls, Seventh Series, Smith	$24.95
4647	**Modern Collector's** Dolls, Eighth Series, Smith	$24.95
4640	Patricia Smith's **Doll Values**, Antique to Modern, 12th Edition	$12.95
3826	Story of **Barbie**, Westenhouser	$19.95
1513	**Teddy Bears & Steiff** Animals, Mandel	$9.95
1817	**Teddy Bears & Steiff** Animals, 2nd Series, Mandel	$19.95
2084	**Teddy Bears, Annalee's & Steiff** Animals, 3rd Series, Mandel	$19.95
1808	Wonder of **Barbie**, Manos	$9.95
1430	World of **Barbie** Dolls, Manos	$9.95

FURNITURE

1457	American **Oak** Furniture, McNerney	$9.95
3716	American **Oak** Furniture, Book II, McNerney	$12.95
1118	Antique **Oak** Furniture, Hill	$7.95
2132	Collector's Encyclopedia of **American** Furniture, Vol. I, Swedberg	$24.95
2271	Collector's Encyclopedia of **American** Furniture, Vol. II, Swedberg	$24.95
3720	Collector's Encyclopedia of **American** Furniture, Vol. III, Swedberg	$24.95
3878	Collector's Guide to **Oak** Furniture, George	$12.95
1755	Furniture of the **Depression Era**, Swedberg	$19.95
3906	**Heywood-Wakefield** Modern Furniture, Rouland	$18.95
1885	**Victorian** Furniture, Our American Heritage, McNerney	$9.95
3829	**Victorian** Furniture, Our American Heritage, Book II, McNerney	$9.95
3869	**Victorian** Furniture books, 2 volume set, McNerney	$19.90

JEWELRY, HATPINS, WATCHES & PURSES

1712	Antique & Collector's **Thimbles** & Accessories, Mathis	$19.95
1748	Antique **Purses**, Revised Second Ed., Holiner	$19.95
1278	Art Nouveau & Art Deco **Jewelry**, Baker	$9.95
4558	**Christmas Pins**, Past and Present, Gallina	$18.95
3875	Collecting Antique **Stickpins**, Kerins	$16.95
3722	Collector's Ency. of **Compacts, Carryalls & Face Powder Boxes**, Mueller	$24.95
4655	Complete Price Guide to **Watches**, #16, Shugart	$26.95
1716	Fifty Years of Collectible **Fashion Jewelry**, 1925-1975, Baker	$19.95
1424	**Hatpins** & Hatpin Holders, Baker	$9.95
4570	Ladies' **Compacts**, Gerson	$24.95
1181	100 Years of Collectible **Jewelry**, 1850-1950, Baker	$9.95
2348	20th Century Fashionable Plastic **Jewelry**, Baker	$19.95
3830	Vintage **Vanity Bags & Purses**, Gerson	$24.95

TOYS, MARBLES & CHRISTMAS COLLECTIBLES

3427	**Advertising Character** Collectibles, Dotz	$17.95
2333	Antique & Collector's **Marbles**, 3rd Ed., Grist	$9.95
3827	Antique & Collector's **Toys**, 1870–1950, Longest	$24.95
3956	Baby Boomer **Games**, Identification & Value Guide, Polizzi	$24.95
3717	**Christmas** Collectibles, 2nd Edition, Whitmyer	$24.95
1752	**Christmas** Ornaments, Lights & Decorations, Johnson	$19.95
4649	Classic Plastic **Model Kits**, Polizzi	$24.95

4559	Collectible **Action Figures**, 2nd Ed., Manos	$17.95
3874	Collectible Coca-Cola Toy **Trucks**, deCourtivron	$24.95
2338	Collector's Encyclopedia of **Disneyana**, Longest, Stern	$24.95
4639	Collector's Guide to **Diecast Toys & Scale Models**, Johnson	$19.95
4651	Collector's Guide to **Tinker Toys**, Strange	$18.95
4566	Collector's Guide to **Tootsietoys**, 2nd Ed., Richter	$19.95
3436	Grist's Big Book of **Marbles**	$19.95
3970	Grist's Machine-Made & Contemporary **Marbles**, 2nd Ed.	$9.95
4569	**Howdy Doody**, Collector's Reference and Trivia Guide, Koch	$16.95
4723	**Matchbox®** Toys, 1948 to 1993, Johnson, 2nd Ed	$18.95
3823	**Mego** Toys, An Illustrated Value Guide, Chrouch	15.95
1540	**Modern Toys** 1930–1980, Baker	$19.95
3888	**Motorcycle** Toys, Antique & Contemporary, Gentry/Downs	$18.95
4728	Schroeder's Collectible **Toys**, Antique to Modern Price Guide, 3rd Ed.	$17.95
1886	Stern's Guide to **Disney** Collectibles	$14.95
2139	Stern's Guide to **Disney** Collectibles, 2nd Series	$14.95
3975	Stern's Guide to **Disney** Collectibles, 3rd Series	$18.95
2028	**Toys**, Antique & Collectible, Longest	$14.95
3979	**Zany Characters** of the Ad World, Lamphier	$16.95

INDIANS, GUNS, KNIVES, TOOLS, PRIMITIVES

1868	Antique **Tools**, Our American Heritage, McNerney	$9.95
2015	Archaic **Indian** Points & Knives, Edler	$14.95
1426	**Arrowheads** & Projectile Points, Hothem	$7.95
4633	**Big Little Books**, Jacobs	$18.95
2279	**Indian** Artifacts of the Midwest, Hothem	$14.95
3885	**Indian** Artifacts of the Midwest, Book II, Hothem	$16.95
1964	**Indian** Axes & Related Stone Artifacts, Hothem	$14.95
2023	**Keen Kutter** Collectibles, Heuring	$14.95
4724	Modern **Guns**, Identification & Values, 11th Ed., Quertermous	$12.95
4505	Standard Guide to **Razors**, Ritchie & Stewart	$9.95
4730	Standard **Knife** Collector's Guide, 3rd Ed., Ritchie & Stewart	$12.95

PAPER COLLECTIBLES & BOOKS

4633	**Big Little Books**, Jacobs	$18.95
1441	Collector's Guide to **Post Cards**, Wood	$9.95
2081	Guide to Collecting **Cookbooks**, Allen	$14.95
4648	Huxford's **Old Book** Value Guide, 8th Ed.	$19.95
2080	Price Guide to **Cookbooks & Recipe Leaflets**, Dickinson	$9.95
2346	**Sheet Music** Reference & Price Guide, 2nd Ed., Pafik & Guiheen	$18.95
4654	**Victorian Trading Cards**, Historical Reference & Value Guide, Cheadle	$19.95

GLASSWARE

1006	**Cambridge Glass** Reprint 1930–1934	$14.95
1007	**Cambridge Glass** Reprint 1949–1953	$14.95
4561	Collectible **Drinking Glasses**, Chase & Kelly	$17.95
4642	Collectible **Glass Shoes**, Wheatley	$19.95
4553	Coll. **Glassware** from the 40's, 50's & 60's, 3rd Ed., Florence	$19.95
2352	Collector's Encyclopedia of **Akro Agate Glassware**, Florence	$14.95
1810	Collector's Encyclopedia of **American Art Glass**, Shuman	$29.95
3312	Collector's Encyclopedia of **Children's Dishes**, Whitmyer	$19.95
4552	Collector's Encyclopedia of **Depression Glass**, 12th Ed., Florence	$19.95
1664	Collector's Encyclopedia of **Heisey Glass**, 1925–1938, Bredehoft	$24.95
3905	Collector's Encyclopedia of **Milk Glass**, Newbound	$24.95
1523	Colors In **Cambridge Glass**, National Cambridge Society	$19.95
4564	**Crackle Glass**, Weitman	$19.95
2275	**Czechoslovakian Glass** and Collectibles, Barta/Rose	$16.95
4714	**Czechoslovakian Glass** and Collectibles, Book II, Barta/Rose	$16.95
4716	**Elegant Glassware** of the Depression Era, 7th Ed., Florence	$19.95
1380	Encylopedia of **Pattern Glass**, McClain	$12.95
3981	Ever's Standard **Cut Glass** Value Guide	$12.95
4659	**Fenton** Art Glass, 1907–1939, Whitmyer	$24.95
3725	**Fostoria**, Pressed, Blown & Hand Molded Shapes, Kerr	$24.95
3883	**Fostoria Stemware**, The Crystal for America, Long & Seate	$24.95
3318	**Glass Animals** of the Depression Era, Garmon & Spencer	$19.95
4644	**Imperial Carnival Glass**, Burns	$18.95

COLLECTOR BOOKS
Informing Today's Collector

3886	Kitchen Glassware of the Depression Years, 5th Ed., Florence	$19.95
2394	Oil Lamps II, Glass Kerosene Lamps, Thuro	$24.95
4725	Pocket Guide to Depression Glass, 10th Ed., Florence	$9.95
4634	Standard Encyclopedia of Carnival Glass, 5th Ed., Edwards	$24.95
4635	Standard Carnival Glass Price Guide, 10th Ed.	$9.95
3974	Standard Encylopedia of Opalescent Glass, Edwards	$19.95
4731	Stemware Identification, Featuring Cordials with Values, Florence	$24.95
3326	Very Rare Glassware of the Depression Years, 3rd Series, Florence	$24.95
3909	Very Rare Glassware of the Depression Years, 4th Series, Florence	$24.95
4732	Very Rare Glassware of the Depression Years, 5th Series, Florence	$24.95
4656	Westmoreland Glass, Wilson	$24.95
2224	World of Salt Shakers, 2nd Ed., Lechner	$24.95

POTTERY

4630	American Limoges, Limoges	$24.95
1312	Blue & White Stoneware, McNerney	$9.95
1958	So. Potteries Blue Ridge Dinnerware, 3rd Ed., Newbound	$14.95
1959	Blue Willow, 2nd Ed., Gaston	$14.95
3816	Collectible Vernon Kilns, Nelson	$24.95
3311	Collecting Yellow Ware – Id. & Value Guide, McAllister	$16.95
1373	Collector's Encyclopedia of American Dinnerware, Cunningham	$24.95
3815	Collector's Encyclopedia of Blue Ridge Dinnerware, Newbound	$19.95
4658	Collector's Encyclopedia of Brush-McCoy Pottery, Huxford	$24.95
2272	Collector's Encyclopedia of California Pottery, Chipman	$24.95
3811	Collector's Encyclopedia of Colorado Pottery, Carlton	$24.95
2133	Collector's Encyclopedia of Cookie Jars, Roerig	$24.95
3723	Collector's Encyclopedia of Cookie Jars, Volume II, Roerig	$24.95
3429	Collector's Encyclopedia of Cowan Pottery, Saloff	$24.95
4638	Collector's Encyclopedia of Dakota Potteries, Dommel	$24.95
2209	Collector's Encyclopedia of Fiesta, 7th Ed., Huxford	$19.95
4718	Collector's Encyclopedia of Figural Planters & Vases, Newbound	$19.95
3961	Collector's Encyclopedia of Early Noritake, Alden	$24.95
1439	Collector's Encyclopedia of Flow Blue China, Gaston	$19.95
3812	Collector's Encyclopedia of Flow Blue China, 2nd Ed., Gaston	$24.95
3813	Collector's Encyclopedia of Hall China, 2nd Ed., Whitmyer	$24.95
3431	Collector's Encyclopedia of Homer Laughlin China, Jasper	$24.95
1276	Collector's Encyclopedia of Hull Pottery, Roberts	$19.95
4573	Collector's Encyclopedia of Knowles, Taylor & Knowles, Gaston	$24.95
3962	Collector's Encyclopedia of Lefton China, DeLozier	$19.95
2210	Collector's Encyclopedia of Limoges Porcelain, 2nd Ed., Gaston	$24.95
2334	Collector's Encyclopedia of Majolica Pottery, Katz-Marks	$19.95
1358	Collector's Encyclopedia of McCoy Pottery, Huxford	$19.95
3963	Collector's Encyclopedia of Metlox Potteries, Gibbs Jr.	$24.95
3313	Collector's Encyclopedia of Niloak, Gifford	$19.95
3837	Collector's Encyclopedia of Nippon Porcelain I, Van Patten	$24.95
2089	Collector's Ency. of Nippon Porcelain, 2nd Series, Van Patten	$24.95
1665	Collector's Ency. of Nippon Porcelain, 3rd Series, Van Patten	$24.95
3836	Nippon Porcelain Price Guide, Van Patten	$9.95
1447	Collector's Encyclopedia of Noritake, Van Patten	$19.95
3432	Collector's Encyclopedia of Noritake, 2nd Series, Van Patten	$24.95
1037	Collector's Encyclopedia of Occupied Japan, Vol. I, Florence	$14.95
1038	Collector's Encyclopedia of Occupied Japan, Vol. II, Florence	$14.95
2088	Collector's Encyclopedia of Occupied Japan, Vol. III, Florence	$14.95
2019	Collector's Encyclopedia of Occupied Japan, Vol. IV, Florence	$14.95
2335	Collector's Encyclopedia of Occupied Japan, Vol. V, Florence	$14.95
3964	Collector's Encyclopedia of Pickard China, Reed	$24.95
1311	Collector's Encyclopedia of R.S. Prussia, 1st Series, Gaston	$24.95
1715	Collector's Encyclopedia of R.S. Prussia, 2nd Series, Gaston	$24.95
3726	Collector's Encyclopedia of R.S. Prussia, 3rd Series, Gaston	$24.95
3877	Collector's Encyclopedia of R.S. Prussia, 4th Series, Gaston	$24.95
1034	Collector's Encyclopedia of Roseville Pottery, Huxford	$19.95
1035	Collector's Encyclopedia of Roseville Pottery, 2nd Ed., Huxford	$19.95
3357	Roseville Price Guide No. 10	$9.95
3965	Collector's Encyclopedia of Sascha Brastoff, Conti, Bethany & Seay	$24.95
3314	Collector's Encyclopedia of Van Briggle Art Pottery, Sasicki	$24.95
4563	Collector's Encyclopedia of Wall Pockets, Newbound	$19.95
2111	Collector's Encyclopedia of Weller Pottery, Huxford	$29.95
3452	Coll. Guide to Country Stoneware & Pottery, Raycraft	$11.95
2077	Coll. Guide to Country Stoneware & Pottery, 2nd Series, Raycraft	$14.95
3434	Coll. Guide to Hull Pottery, The Dinnerware Line, Gick-Burke	$16.95

3876	Collector's Guide to Lu-Ray Pastels, Meehan	$18.95
3814	Collector's Guide to Made in Japan Ceramics, White	$18.95
4646	Collector's Guide to Made in Japan Ceramics, Book II, White	$18.95
4565	Collector's Guide to Rockingham, The Enduring Ware, Brewer	$14.95
2339	Collector's Guide to Shawnee Pottery, Vanderbilt	$19.95
1425	Cookie Jars, Westfall	$9.95
3440	Cookie Jars, Book II, Westfall	$19.95
3435	Debolt's Dictionary of American Pottery Marks	$17.95
2379	Lehner's Ency. of U.S. Marks on Pottery, Porcelain & China	$24.95
4722	McCoy Pottery, Collector's Reference & Value Guide, Hanson/Nissen	$19.95
3825	Puritan Pottery, Morris	$24.95
4726	Red Wing Art Pottery, 1920s–1960s, Dollen	$19.95
1670	Red Wing Collectibles, DePasquale	$9.95
1440	Red Wing Stoneware, DePasquale	$9.95
3738	Shawnee Pottery, Mangus	$24.95
4629	Turn of the Century American Dinnerware, 1880s–1920s, Jasper	$24.95
4572	Wall Pockets of the Past, Perkins	$17.95
3327	Watt Pottery – Identification & Value Guide, Morris	$19.95

OTHER COLLECTIBLES

4704	Antique & Collectible Buttons, Wisniewski	$19.95
2269	Antique Brass & Copper Collectibles, Gaston	$16.95
1880	Antique Iron, McNerney	$9.95
3872	Antique Tins, Dodge	$24.95
1714	Black Collectibles, Gibbs	$19.95
1128	Bottle Pricing Guide, 3rd Ed., Cleveland	$7.95
4636	Celluloid Collectibles, Dunn	$14.95
3959	Cereal Box Bonanza, The 1950's, Bruce	$19.95
3718	Collectible Aluminum, Grist	$16.95
3445	Collectible Cats, An Identification & Value Guide, Fyke	$18.95
4560	Collectible Cats, An Identification & Value Guide, Book II, Fyke	$19.95
1634	Collector's Ency. of Figural & Novelty Salt & Pepper Shakers, Davern	$19.95
2020	Collector's Ency. of Figural & Novelty Salt & Pepper Shakers, Vol. II, Davern	$19.95
2018	Collector's Encyclopedia of Granite Ware, Greguire	$24.95
3430	Collector's Encyclopedia of Granite Ware, Book II, Greguire	$24.95
4705	Collector's Guide to Antique Radios, 4th Ed., Bunis	$18.95
1916	Collector's Guide to Art Deco, Gaston	$14.95
3880	Collector's Guide to Cigarette Lighters, Flanagan	$17.95
4637	Collector's Guide to Cigarette Lighters, Book II, Flanagan	$17.95
1537	Collector's Guide to Country Baskets, Raycraft	$9.95
3966	Collector's Guide to Inkwells, Identification & Values, Badders	$18.95
3881	Collector's Guide to Novelty Radios, Bunis/Breed	$18.95
4652	Collector's Guide to Transistor Radios, 2nd Ed., Bunis	$16.95
4653	Collector's Guide to TV Memorabilia, 1960s–1970s, Davis/Morgan	$24.95
2276	Decoys, Kangas	$24.95
1629	Doorstops, Identification & Values, Bertoia	$9.95
4567	Figural Napkin Rings, Gottschalk & Whitson	$18.95
3968	Fishing Lure Collectibles, Murphy/Edmisten	$24.95
3817	Flea Market Trader, 10th Ed., Huxford	$12.95
3976	Foremost Guide to Uncle Sam Collectibles, Czulewicz	$24.95
4641	Garage Sale & Flea Market Annual, 4th Ed.	$19.95
3819	General Store Collectibles, Wilson	$24.95
4643	Great American West Collectibles, Wilson	$24.95
2215	Goldstein's Coca-Cola Collectibles	$16.95
3884	Huxford's Collectible Advertising, 2nd Ed.	$24.95
2216	Kitchen Antiques, 1790–1940, McNerney	$14.95
3321	Ornamental & Figural Nutcrackers, Rittenhouse	$16.95
2026	Railroad Collectibles, 4th Ed., Baker	$14.95
1632	Salt & Pepper Shakers, Guarnaccia	$9.95
1888	Salt & Pepper Shakers II, Identification & Value Guide, Book II, Guarnaccia	$14.95
2220	Salt & Pepper Shakers III, Guarnaccia	$14.95
3443	Salt & Pepper Shakers IV, Guarnaccia	$18.95
4555	Schroeder's Antiques Price Guide, 14th Ed., Huxford	$12.95
2096	Silverplated Flatware, Revised 4th Edition, Hagan	$14.95
1922	Standard Old Bottle Price Guide, Sellari	$14.95
4708	Summers' Guide to Coca-Cola	$19.95
3892	Toy & Miniature Sewing Machines, Thomas	$18.95
3828	Value Guide to Advertising Memorabilia, Summers	$18.95
3977	Value Guide to Gas Station Memorabilia, Summers & Priddy	$24.95
3444	Wanted to Buy, 5th Edition	$9.95

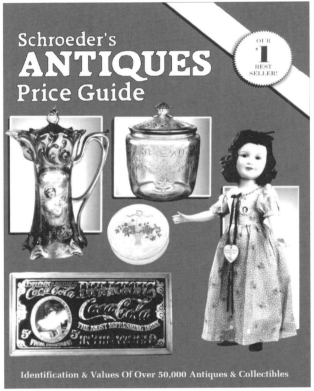